NEW TECHNIQUES FOR CATCHING BOTTOM FISH

In Washington, British Columbia, Oregon, California & Alaskan Waters

Doug Wilson and Fred Vander Werff

The Writing Works
Division of Morse Press
Seattle, Washington

Library of Congress Cataloging in Publication Data

Wilson, Doug
New techniques for catching bottom fish in Washington,
Oregon, British Columbia, California, and Alaska

Includes index.
1. Salt water fishing—Northwest, Pacific. I. Vander Werff,
Fred, joint author. II. Title. New Techniques for catching bottom
fish . . .
SH464.N6W54   1977   799.1′66′63   77-17923
ISBN 0-916076-16-4

Library of Congress Catalog Card Number: 77-17923

Foreword

FOR THE PAST four years, my job has been the research, promotion and promulgation of information on recreational fisheries for the numerous bottom species found in Puget Sound, Washington. During the course of my work, it has been my great pleasure to have a working and fishing relationship with the authors of this book. As authors of one of the few "how-to" books on northwest bottom fishing, Fred Vander Werff and Doug Wilson included information, concepts and attitudes that only could come from an intimate knowledge and a heartfelt relationship with this great resource.

Fred's work background with my program and Doug's as a commercial bottom fisherman, do, I feel, give them the special qualifications needed to comment on the feeding habits of various rockfish, fishing techniques, preservation of catch and resource conservation.

Doubtless, more books on bottom fishing will be available in time, but this work will be the standard for years to come.

Percy M. Washington
Fishery Research Biologist
NWAFC, NMFS

For Diane and Helen

Contents

Preface

THE PURPOSE of writing this book is to help fishermen catch more bottom fish.

Here in the Pacific Northwest, anglers have access to a great many bottom species from small perch and flatfishes to large rockfishes in the 20-pound class. Ling Cod attain weights in excess of 60 pounds. Pacific Halibut reach 200 pounds. Many species may be taken on gear ranging from ultra-light to wire-line-rigged boat rods required to handle some of the larger bottom species.

The importance of the Pacific Northwest bottom fish fishery has always been overshadowed by the glamour species of the northwest waters, salmon and steelhead trout. Both species, along with other trout found in salt water during certain periods of their life cycle, are great gamefish. However, since they tend to be migratory and seasonally abundant, they are more difficult to catch by most anglers.

Bottom fish offer an alternative fishing challenge. They are available at all seasons of the year, eagerly attack a variety of lures and bait, are sporty on the right tackle, and last but not least, absolutely delicious on the table.

Despite the availability of our bottom fish resources, many anglers lack the knowledge of consistently productive bottom fishing techniques, taking most bottom fish incidental to salmon fishing activity.

It is the author's hope that this book will provide northwest salt-water anglers with the basic guidelines for bottom fishing, which should result in larger, more consistent catches, hours of greater fishing pleasure, and an appreciation of the sport that bottom fish can provide when taken on tackle matched to the fishing conditions and the types of fish taken.

Bottom fish are often classified as nonfighters because the tackle used is too overpowering. This book outlines some techniques and methods that can quickly change an angler's attitude toward the fighting ability of bottom species, as well as help to increase his catches.

Your first encounter with a 3-pound Black Rockfish taken on light spinning tackle or an attempt to work a good-sized Ling Cod from its rocky lair 120 feet beneath the surface on standard steelhead fishing gear will likely astound you and may likely convert you to a dedicated bottom fisherman on the spot.

It is our hope that this will be the case.

We furthermore hope that if you become a dedicated bottom fisherman, you treat this valuable resource with respect and concern for its future.

Bottom fish are often thought of as being in endless supply. Like every other resource, if it is abused, it can be severely depleted. Certain traditional bottom fishing areas have actually been over-fished to the point of unproductivity. Rockfish exhibit slow growth and long life cycles and are susceptible to heavy angling pressure. Copper Rockfish in the 2- to 3-pound class can easily be 10 or 12 years old. An extremely large Copper Rockfish might be as much as 25 years old.

Appreciate this resource; take only as much as you can reasonably use, regardless of legal catch limits. Take care of your catch, and don't waste it.

The fish you leave today will be there for your sport tomorrow and for the generations of anglers that follow you.

Wishing you tight lines.

Fred Vander Werff
Doug Wilson

1

Bottom Fishing for Sport and Eating

UNTIL the last few years, fishermen along the Pacific Coast from nothern California to Alaska have said few kind words about bottom fish. With salmon being THE FISH, rockfish and cod have been scorned as "scrap fish."

In the early sixties when we frequently trolled for salmon on the northern California Coast from the ports of Eureka and Trinidad, we also had few kind words for the hordes of Black Rockfish we would encounter on the salmon grounds.

Terminal trolling tackle in this coastal area consisted of a flasher with sinker release and 3-pound, cannon-ball lead. Being such voracious feeders, a school of hungry Blacks could wipe us out of bait and weights in short order. Our only option was to pull up and run somewhere else to get back into the salmon. Had we known then what we know today, we wouldn't have run anywhere. We'd have quickly exchanged our heavy salmon trolling rigs for light casting rods and leadhead jigs. Within moments of our first casts, we'd

1

be hollering with joy as we battled 3- to 5-pound scrappers slamming our jigs on every cast!

We'd bet that by the time we had our third hookup, our diehard salmon fishing buddies would be eagerly reaching for our rods and saying, "Hey, let me try that!"

Bottom fish are so much fun on the right tackle with the proper lures that you'll find yourself ready to spend most of your time bottom fishing. You'll seek salmon only during the time and tide periods that promise optimum salmon fishing opportunities. You'll have more fun, be able to spend more time productively fishing, and end up with a fish box full of some very fine eating.

Salmon tend to be migratory. Even when locally abundant, salmon usually bite only during the early and late evening hours or just on the turn of the tide. Bottom fish, on the other hand, are available in the same localities year 'round and are readily waiting to strike if you've got the know-how to fish for them.

During this same time period when we fished the northern California Coast, attitudes toward bottom fish were negative along the entire North Pacific Coast—and in some places still are. At Neah Bay, Washington fishermen were frequently warned, "Stay away from Duncan Rock. You can't make a pass by there without getting a sea bass (Black Rockfish) on every line."

On a good summer weekend nowadays, staying away from Duncan Rock may be easier than it was not too many years ago. In fact you may have trouble getting near it because of the crowd of boats around it!

Times are changing, and bottom fish have found some advocates in the fishing fraternity. Cleaning tables at boat docks where once a pile of rockfish would draw the comment, "Oh, just rockfish, where'd you catch 'em?," now draws excited questions by anglers anxious to set their hooks into several of the husky scrappers. Occasionally some old diehard salmon fisherman will even comment, "You know, they don't fight much, but I'd rather eat bottom fish than salmon any day."

He could be only half right. The eating comment is only half the true story on bottom fish. Matched with the right tackle, a salmon fisherman will be amazed at how hard rockfish fight.

You don't hunt rabbits with an elephant gun; the same principle applies to bottom fish.

Most bottom fish are still caught using herring and salmon style hookups, primarily because most fishermen seek bottom fish the same way they mooch for salmon.

A fantastic breakthrough in bottom fishing techniques has evolved from research. These techniques,

Standard steelhead casting rods and level wind reels are ideal for casting leadhead jigs and other lightweight artificial lures. Don Dudley (left) and Fred Vander Werff are the fishermen.

new to Pacific Northwest waters, use leadhead jigs and plastic worms. They will amaze even dedicated bottom fishermen, who have been using standard bait or jigging techniques. Originally developed for fresh-water bass fishing and refined from jigs with pork rind, the leadhead jigs and plastic worms provide an entirely new approach to shallow-water bottom fishing.

This method is so effective that it has been used extensively in Puget Sound by the National Marine Fisheries Game Fish Project and Washington State Fisheries to collect bottom fish for tagging studies. More recently the Seattle Aquarium has used shallow-water fishing techniques with leadhead jigs and plastic worms to collect display fish.

Black or Yellowtail Rockfish are frequently found in schools feeding on or near the surface in shallow water. A light steelhead rod or bass casting rod with

Black Rockfish are aggressive feeders that readily strike a variety of lures. These scrappers weigh an average of three to four pounds.

A 1/2-ounce leadhead jig with bucktail and weedguard and 6-inch black plastic worm is one of the most productive shallow water bottom-fishing lures a salt-water angler can carry in his tackle-box.

jigs will bring strikes so fast and furiously you'll be wondering why you've never found the fish like this before.

With a medium-weight 8-foot steelhead rod rigged with a 1 1/2 ounce *Hopkins Hammertail* jig and gold-flecked, 6-inch plastic worm, we've drifted through a school of Black Rockfish at the kelp's edge on the Washington Coast where 12 casts produced 12 straight hookups.

Unusual? Hardly. Earlier in the morning we had hit into a school of surface-feeding Blacks. With three of us casting, we stayed constantly hooked up to fish for 30 minutes before we wore out our wrists landing and releasing Blacks as fast as we could cast and land them. At the time, a southwesterly 15-knot wind was buffeting us, and we were bouncing in a 4-foot chop with the rain pelting down.

These are not the kind of conditions that normally are considered ideal for fishing. If we'd been fishing herring, we would have drifted too fast in the wind to fish successfully.

With our light casting rods and 1/2-ounce bucktail jigs with 6-inch black curly-tailed worms we could cast far from the boat in the direction we were drifting. We quickly began retrieving line with short uplifting strokes of the rod tip to impart a fluttering action in our jigs. Almost immediately we received a strike on every cast as long as we stayed with the school. Despite unfavorable weather conditions, we caught and released about 30 rockfish in 30 minutes.

The secret to our success was simple—knowledge of proper rockfish habitat and lures that yield the greatest efficiency in fishing results.

While salmon are fast-moving fish and charge through baitfish, most rockfish tend to lie in wait and make a short dash to grab the unsuspecting prey. Black and Yellowtail Rockfish do feed on small herring; however, they and other rockfish ambush their prey from close range.

By concentrating on shallow-water fishing, we've found that we can easily catch whatever fish we want for our table, have more fun doing it, and are frequently able to go fishing more often by taking shorter but very productive trips.

It's not uncommon to trailer our boats after work to Puget Sound, where we live, and fish for a few hours on a summer evening. This way we can fish several times a month instead of having to plan elaborate trips that allow us to go only on days off.

WOMEN AND KIDS

Another beautiful quality of the light tackle and shallow-water fishing—they are perfectly suited to women and children. A medium- to light-spinning outfit does not require the muscle of an NFL linebacker to handle it effectively and catch bottom fish. We have converted both of our wives, previously lukewarm about fishing, into dedicated bottom fishers. This can become habit-forming, however, and your days of

Diane Wilson with a China Rockfish caught in 30 feet of water at the kelp's edge along Waadah Island at Neah Bay, Washington.

sneaking off with your fishing buddies may be numbered.

Light tackle and shallow-water fishing offer an excellent opportunity to teach youngsters how to fish. Choose a previously scouted, never-fail bottom fish spot to introduce the kids to fishing. Equip them with tackle they can handle, and don't expect to do a lot of fishing yourself. If you choose the right spot and conditions, you won't have time to fish yourself, because you'll be too busy unhooking fish and helping the kids. Teaching kids how to fish should be handled carefully. We've found that the best procedure is to show them how to do it one time. After that advise sparingly and encourage often. Too much advice or criticism can stifle youthful enthusiasm. Young fishermen are turned off if adults are too demanding. The secret for developing young fishing companions—enough action to maintain their interest, short trips, and patience. Don't expect expertise on the first trip. Remembering these few pointers will lead to dedicated young anglers that will make any parent proud.

BOTTOM FISHING—THE FLEXIBLE SPORT

Once you've learned to locate proper habitat, pick optimum tides, and use the most effective lures properly, shallow water rockfishing can become your most effective and funfilled salt-water fishing.

Bottom fishing situations can be divided into a diverse category with each requiring certain techniques for the most efficient fishing.

Shallow-water fishing can be done by boat or from shore. The coastline from California to Alaska offers thousands of miles of rock and shore fishing shallows. Jetties line the entrance of many of the coast's harbors and present another opportunity for the rock-hopping bottom fisherman.

Fishing from jetties in northern California, we frequently hooked fish that bore off with such power that we could not stop their dogged runs, which abruptly ended in some underwater cave or crevice. There our lines were hopelessly fouled, and breaking off was the only answer. Since we were never successful in stopping one of these, we could never be sure of the fish at the other end. We were likely tying into large Cabezon. The surge of power we encountered was typical of the fight put up by the many Cabezon we'd boated on Puget Sound and Washington coastal waters. Both Cabezon and rockfishes develop stout strong bodies capable of surprisingly strong but fairly short runs.

In slinging 1/4-ounce jigs and plastic worms from the rocky shoreline at Depoe Bay, Oregon, we found that we could land hard-running Blue Rockfish, a fish often mistaken for Black Rockfish. We were using light spinning tackle and waiting for the waves to help us lift our fish up the rock ledge where we could land them. We were hooking and landing the Blues and Ling Cod within 100 feet of U.S. Highway 101, the main street of this small fishing community, famous for salmon and bottom fishing charters. However, our effectiveness would have tripled had we been using our two-handled steelhead casting rods. We had left them home on this trip because we had not originally included a stop on the coast. Fortunately, we had some jigs in our gear among the freshwater lures we were packing.

From the number of fellow tourists that gathered to question us about our catch as we walked back to the car, it was apparent to us that many of them would enjoy the opportunity we had taken advantage of only too briefly. The area offers many miles of shoreline fishing possibilities. If you are traveling to the coast and your schedule does not permit time to go fishing by private or charter boat, don't overlook the opportunities for shore fishing.

Finding such a productive fishing spot where we

saw no other shorebound anglers that day points out the necessity of knowing where to look for fish. Understanding a fish's habitat needs will eliminate much wasted time.

When we spotted the section of rocky shoreline which obviously was several feet deep right at the water's edge, we knew that we had a likely spot to try. We quickly confirmed it by hooking a fish on the second cast. Enough action followed in the next half hour to provide a couple of fish dinners.

Once we had our fish on the rocks, our next actions were equally important to the fulfillment of a good fishing experience—eating our catch. We immediately bled the fish and had them on ice in our chest in the car within minutes of catching. Later, we'll go into greater detail on care and handling of fish after we've covered the numerous techniques used to catch the dozen or so bottom fishes from our coastal waters.

Along with fishing from shore, calmer waters among the islands in Washington's Puget Sound and British Columbia and Alaska's inside coastline can successfully be fished with skiff and cartop boats where access is possible. The bays of many harbors along the coastline from California to Alaska also produce bottom fish. The open ocean offers much shallow-water boat fishing along the shorelines. Surface-feeding Black and Yellowtail Rockfish may be caught miles off shore as well as near the shoreline.

We've fished plastic worm-leadhead jig combinations from cartoppers, piers and jetties, shorelines, and in the open ocean from Oregon to British Columbia in testing. We have consistently come up with the same results.

Jigs and plastic worms outfish bait on shallow water rockfishes at least 5 to 1. The secret seems to be the curly-tailed plastic worm! Standard feathered leadhead jigs alone are less effective than those with a worm added! The undulating tail movement of the worm adds that ingredient that must spell "FOOD" in capital letters to the hungry rockfish waiting for his next morsel to swim along.

The lures simulate the action of many of the major sources of food for bottom fish: small crabs, blennies, gunnels, and small fishes such as sculpins.

Since most bottom fish lie on or near the bottom looking up, anything that appears to be food swimming overhead becomes a likely target. Leadhead jigs rigged with bucktail or plastic skirts and plastic worms create that appetizing silhouette.

In 30 to 40 feet of water, this jig combination is murder on Copper Rockfish. Moving a bit deeper to about 60 to 100 feet, Quillback and Brown Rockfish will start to show up in the fish box. Yellowtail and Blacks are liable to be at any of these depths—or on the surface!

Pacific Cod, when in shallow water during the fall and winter through early spring months, will readily grab these jigs. The new method is far more sporty than the traditional jigging of a hefty 1-pound nordic jig—for years the accepted method to jig for cod.

The best part about fishing with these jigs is—if

Plastic curly-tailed worms give leadhead jigs the action that draws strikes.

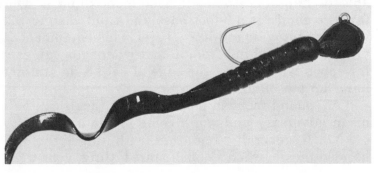

Cabezon, like most bottom fish, lie on or near the bottom waiting for prey. Cabezon feed mainly on crabs.

you already own a medium-weight mooching or steelhead rod and reel capable of casting these light jigs or even your lightweight tackle used for trout fishing, you've got everything you need except the jigs—to catch more fish and have more fun.

We've used everything from ultralight spinning rods and standard bass casting rods and reels to light mooching gear equipped with good casting reels capable of handling 15-pound test monofilament. Our favorite choice is a 6-foot bass and trout casting rod with an *Ambassador 5000 D* reel. This equipment is primarily for fishing from a boat where you can cast into open water along the edge of kelp beds and not hang up too often.

A 3-pound rockfish played on this tackle can be a mean adversary and won't come to the boat easily.

You'll generally find that with this light one-handed tackle, when the fish start hitting, your wrist

A Copper Rockfish ready to land after it slammed a leadhead jig and plastic worm combination in 30 feet of water in Puget Sound.

can't take too much of the tension and strain. You'll most likely have to switch to heavier two-handed casting or spinning rods in self defense.

We've found shallow-water bottom fishing to be more productive than the traditional concept of fishing deep for the bottom fish that prevail in our waters.

Fish hooked with jigs are normally hooked in the edge of the mouth where they can easily be released. By fishing in shallow water, we can safely release the fish after landing it and know that the fish will most likely survive to strike again another day.

If you're fishing in water deeper than 30 or 40 feet, plan on keeping your catch. Fish taken from about 60 feet down or deeper will normally rupture their air bladder by the pressure change of being brought up from depth and will die. When you start fishing in depths to 60 feet or more, definitely plan to kill whatever fish you catch. To throw them back with a

Going deeper can mean bigger fish, especially the red colored species such as the Canary Rockfish.

damaged air bladder wastes a valuable resource.

We feel that some of your greatest bottom fishing thrills are going to come from using these shallow-water techniques. Bottom fishing with sports tackle can be accomplished at depths which we've divided into shallow water (0-40 feet), mid-depth (40-200 feet), and deep water (200-400 feet). We have covered in detail fishing techniques for all depths to 400 feet.

Going deeper can mean bigger fish, particularly for the red-colored rockfishes, which are seldom found shallower than 80 feet, even in northern waters, and usually considerably deeper. Ling Cod and Halibut are taken from about the beginning of the mid-depth range to as deep as you can fish sports tackle, including the use of heavy-duty rods and reels rigged with braided wire line and cannon-ball leads to 64 ounces.

While we prefer to stay with artificial lures in shallow-water fishing, both jigs and bait have their applications in mid-depth to deep-water fishing. We have covered in detail both methods to give you the greatest opportunity to use your fishing time most productively. To fish deep water will require the investment in heavier tackle if you do not already have it for salmon fishing. The same is true of rods and reels for special techniques often required for rock and jetty fishing. There long rods are preferred to give you the reach and leverage needed in fishing among rocks and heavy kelp concentrations where you must be able to tightly control a hooked fish.

As you work your way through this book and learn more about angling for bottom fish, we hope that you'll learn to appreciate this valuable resource. Enjoy it and treasure it, taking only what you can use.

One additional thought we'd like to share as we venture into the world of the avid bottom fisherman: Regardless of where or how you fish for rockfish and other bottom fish, one of the most important factors to be considered is safety. Respect the ocean and don't take chances. Too many inexperienced rock fishermen get swept off their perches by a wave that was just a little bigger than the others breaking on shore. Cartop boats are fine for near-shore fishing in calm water, but it's no fun to be caught in open water with a long run back to the boat ramp in an unexpected wind that

Ling Cod are taken from about the middepth to as deep as you can fish sports tackle.

turned the mirrorlike calmness of early morning into a frothing chop in a matter of minutes. Carry common sense along with your other equipment when going fishing. It can mean the difference in being around to fish another day.

China Rockfish and Kelp Greenling are but two of the shallow water scrappers found along the northern Washington coast.

2
Finding the Fish

Y OUR FIRST PROBLEM as a sports fisherman is to locate your quarry. The key for locating any fish is knowing their habitat. All fish are found in certain areas because the habitat suits their biological requirements. It is not necessary to know all of these requirements, but only what to look for in bottom types. Bottom fish can be classified by their preference to bottom structure. The rockfishes are found on rocky or hard bottom types; the same is true for codfish. Flounders like muddy bottom; perch abound near sloping beaches, eel grass beds, and piers. Greenling and Ling Cod are found on rocky areas and around kelp beds. These requirements cannot be over emphasized. All the fancy techniques and most expensive tackle will not catch fish if used in the wrong areas.

How do you find productive areas? First get a nautical chart of the area you intend to fish. Get the largest scale possible which will have the best detail and definition of the bottom contours. The bottom type is printed on the map. For example, let's look for a

17

A school of Black Rockfish in a kelp bed. Blacks are frequently found off the bottom or in some cases right on the surface.

good rockfish spot. The key items to look for are the areas that are rocky, usually abbreviated "rky." Second, look for some outstanding feature. Kelp beds, pilings, and steep drop-offs are examples of irregularities on an otherwise routine bottom that may be ideal hiding places for fish. Look for areas that are shallower or deeper than surrounding areas. Points of land that drop off sharply on the sides are areas to check out. When areas are found on the map that have possibilities, mark them with a yellow or red feltpen, preferably waterproof. Mark at least six spots to fish, so your chances of finding the fish are maximized.

If possible, talk to someone that knows the area. Bottom fish areas are not usually guarded with the tenacity of good salmon or steelhead spots. Marina operators are good contacts. It's their business to know where to catch fish. Some years ago, that would not have been a good suggestion, because bottom fish were rated one notch below crab bait. During those

Kelp beds are likely locations for most shallow water bottom fish.

times it was our experience that such questions would be hazardous to your health. However, there was never a shortage of questions around the cleaning tables while fileting a good pile of rockfish. Fortunately, more people are becoming enlightened to the fact that fish are fun to catch no matter what their species.

Tackle shops can be another source of reasonably reliable information. Operators hear a lot of fishing talk and are usually good fishermen themselves. When talking to people about fishing areas, ask your source to pinpoint hot spots. You may have overlooked some areas, or they are not obvious on the map.

Boat docks, where successful fishermen return, are another place to pick up information. Sometimes fishermen are vague about the specific location, but knowing the general area is at least a place to start.

Keep in mind that some of the best bottom fishing areas are not well known and some have yet to be discovered. Do your homework and learn productive areas, but spend some time looking for new ones. You may find places that are better than those that are locally regarded as the hot spots.

Conversation and poring over maps are necessary prerequisites, but ultimately, only by going fishing can you verify your ideas. Bear in mind that the best fish finder you have is lodged firmly between your ears. Think about the fish you expect to catch, and find out all you can about their habits and feeding patterns. If you have salmon fishing experience, try to forget it. Bottom fish are totally different critters. Salmon chase their prey and will wander great distances. With few exceptions bottom fish ambush their prey from close range and are usually found in the same spot day after day.

Now that you are ready to go fishing, pick a day when the tidal exchange is minimal. Tide books and calendars list high and low tides for a month at a time. Look for the days when there is less than one foot per hour ebb or flood of the tide. The direction of tidal flow is not as important as how fast it runs. Bottom dwelling species are flattened against the bottom in extreme currents and usually will not be active lest they lose their position. Midwater species are not so adversely affected by tidal changes. In rapid tidal flow it's difficult to get your lure or bait to the bottom and keep it there. It is also difficult to keep your boat from drifting too fast.

Now you have your date to go fishing and your map in hand. After you launch your boat and while you cruise to the chosen fishing area, observe the wind direction and tide flow. When you get to your desig-

Pacific Cod

nated area, study the contour of the land beyond the beach. Ridges and valleys often extend beyond the waterline. These are the features that could lead to finding a hot spot.

If you're looking for shallow-water rockfish and Pacific Cod hot spots, look on the beach for rocky patches at the water's edge. Also look for rocky ridges that extend into the water. Unless you specifically want to catch flounder, don't waste your time with areas that have mud or sand beaches with little slope to them. Kelp beds are giveaways to hard-bottom fishing spots. The kelp must have a solid substrate on which to anchor itself. If you don't find fish in the kelp, search further away in deeper water; chances are good the bottom is still hard.

Once you're away from shallow water areas along rocky shorelines and kelp beds, finding the fish becomes a game of chance.

Using charts and reference points to get over well-known bottom fishing areas is a start. A depth sounder will greatly aid your efforts. With good charts and a depth sounder that reads from 0 to 60 fathoms (most models come as 60 feet-60 fathom reading units), you can locate drop-offs and contours on the bottom that will indicate likely spots to locate bottom fish.

If you have a very sophisticated and expensive sounder, you may on occasion spot schools of fish with your sounder if they are off the bottom a ways. The key use of a depth sounder, however, is to read the bottom—its depth and contour lines.

A depth finder with flasher type recording gear will read a muddy bottom as a wide, flat band, a rocky or hard smooth bottom with a narrow band, and jagged, rocky bottom with several narrow bands. Study the operator's manual that is supplied with every depth sounder for complete explanation of the signals on the dial.

By using charts indicating approximate depths of local hot spots, which are available at nearly any resort or boat house in the area you'll be fishing, you can locate the general area, then start pinpointing drop-offs, depressions, and ridges where bottom fish tend to congregate. With a sounder, you'll be surprised how much a bottom will vary within a fairly small sector of water.

Fish where you find depressions and ridges, edges of drop-offs, and/or irregular sections of bottom for your best chances of finding fish.

By using a sounder, we've found that you can spend more time working a potentially productive area, and not waste time hitting spots that turn out to be so deep that you can't get your gear down or so shallow that you should be using lighter, shallow-water gear and techniques.

In some spots in Puget Sound a drop-off edge literally drops away from 10 or 15 fathoms to 60 in a matter of yards. The Straits of Juan de Fuca have shoals and sandbars that come up within a few fathoms of the surface far from the shoreline.

Without a sounder you'll find yourself perplexed when you drop your lines guessing that it is 100 or so feet deep, only to see 200 yards of line peel off. This leaves you with an empty spool and still no sign of bottom. Equally perplexing is the exact opposite where you're geared up to fish deep using heavy leads and find that you're 2 miles off shore but only in 60 feet of water. Here 3 ounces of lead will be more than adequate even with some tidal flow.

Having fished without the benefit of a sounder for several years in the Puget Sound area, it came as a pleasant surprise when, on the first trip out with a sounder, we located a Yelloweye Rockfish bed in 40 fathoms of water. This area was reputed to hold these fish, but we had been unsuccessful in locating them over a period of two years of sporadically attempting to pinpoint the spot in Possession Sound south of Mukilteo.

In an area that the charts indicated was 80 fathoms deep, we found a shelf that rose up to 15 fathoms at its southeast corner, dropped to 22 fathoms on the north end, and from 22 to 35, then 40 fathoms on the western side of the shelf, which was less than a quarter-mile long and 300 yards wide.

When we passed from the 35 to 40 fathom mark, we immediately began hooking Yelloweyes. As quickly as we drifted through this drop-off point and hooked a fish, the bottom would go completely off the scope. The depth was beyond the ability of our sounder to read, indicating it was probably about the 80 fathoms noted on the charts.

As soon as we could pump up our fish, we'd work our way back up over the edge of the shelf to about 25 fathoms, drop our gear and drift back over the edge of the shelf. Immediately we hooked up again. We repeated until we had caught enough Yelloweyes for several meals.

After carefully charting this spot during several trips, we found that the Yelloweye hot spot couldn't be more than 40 yards wide. Luck, the right tide, and the depth sounder gave us a chance to sink hooks into these delicious rockfish, which average around 10 pounds. They are such a valuable resource among our bottom fishes, we limit our catch from 1 to 3 Yelloweye per trip so as not to over-fish the school.

Sounders for effective midwater and deep-water fishing in the 60 feet-60 fathom models can be purchased for about $200 to $400, depending on brands. Coastal Navigator, made in Seattle, is widely accepted. Lowrance, made in Tulsa, Oklahoma, is also a good unit. If cost is no consideration, Ross of Seattle makes a high quality unit.

After searching with depth sounder and checking by looking at the shore, move your boat up wind or tide from where you suspect the fish will be and commence fishing. Keep drifting over the area until you find fish or determine it is unproductive. Finding fish is a searching procedure, so move around without stopping until you have pinpointed a good spot. When you hook your first fish in a new area, immediately look for solid landmarks so you can move back to the exact spot. The best procedure is to line up two stable objects on the land: towers, houses, roads, antennas, trees, and chimneys are good examples. Don't use moored boats, parked cars, buoys, and the like. The next time you want to find your honey hole, the landmarks may have moved, leaving you to find it all over again. Then look 90 degrees from those landmarks you've noted and line up two more. You now have the exact spot located at the intersection of the two sight lines. Navigational and mooring buoys may shift their position several yards during tide changes. Worse yet, navigational buoys may be occasionally relocated, and the marker you've depended on no longer marks your hot spot. Buoy changes have occurred at LaPush, Washington in recent years.

When searching for fish in water up to 100 feet deep, artificial lures offer many advantages over bait. Most lures can be cast and worked back to the boat effectively. If fishing in shallow to mid-depths, consider the area sampled versus mooching bait along the path of your drift. By casting away from the path of your boat, you are effectively searching the greatest area possible.

Some very productive bottom fish lures are bucktail jig and pork rind, leadhead jigs, and curly-tail plastic worms, and various jigging spoons such as *Hopkins, Stingsilda,* and *Buzz-bomb.* Match your lure weight to the depth and type of bottom cover you're fishing. Kelp beds and shallow rocky areas up to 40 feet deep are best worked with 1/2-to 1-ounce leadhead jigs with various trailers. These lures ride over the bottom and through weeds with the single hook riding upright to minimize hang-ups. Use the lightest lure weight possible and still get to the bottom. Heavy lures in shallow water lead to many hang-ups and lost lures. When fishing deeper than 40 feet, use heavier leadheads, 1 to 3 ounces, and the jigging spoons 2 to 7 ounces. We'll go into complete discussion of techniques in the chapters on fishing shallow and medium depths. Good bottom fish lures are designed to bounce on the bottom. This will tell you something about its features. A good bottom jigger will learn the area much faster than a fisherman who drifts his bait above the bottom. You should know whether the bottom is hard or soft. If you are searching for rockfish, finding a small patch of jumbled boulders can spell the difference between success and failure.

Artificial lures are designed to be worked by the fisherman. Therefore, you must stay alert and concentrate on what your lure is doing. Mooching bait is relaxing but doesn't allow intimate contact with the bottom on every cast. Another useful tip: use tackle only heavy enough to land your desired quarry. Tackle for bottom fish is often stereotyped into the heavy boat rods and mule-tripping line strength category. Line testing 12- to 20-pound test will allow lures to sink faster and deeper. Lures also act more effectively when tied to more flexible, smaller diameter line. Lighter rods provide more sensitive feel, useful in determining bottom type and subtle strikes. You will also enjoy more sport on lighter tackle.

Remember, finding bottom fish is a searching game. Don't spend all day in an area if it's not producing. Go find the fish. Search different depths, and use effective lures. Bottom fish are not very choosy when it comes to lures, and many methods are productive. But, use methods that cover a lot of water. When the fish are located, slow down and work the area thoroughly. If the fish are found on a certain bottom type, look around for the same characteristics in other areas. Chances are good they will also be fishy.

A variety of jigging lures for water deeper than 40 feet that are excellent producers are, from top to bottom, *Hopkins NO-EQL* jigging spoons in 2 oz. and 3 1/4 oz. weights, *Stingsilda, Hopkins NO-EQL* with swimming tail, *Hopkins Hammertail* with swimming tail.

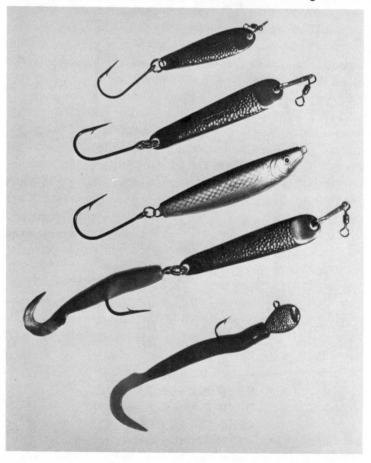

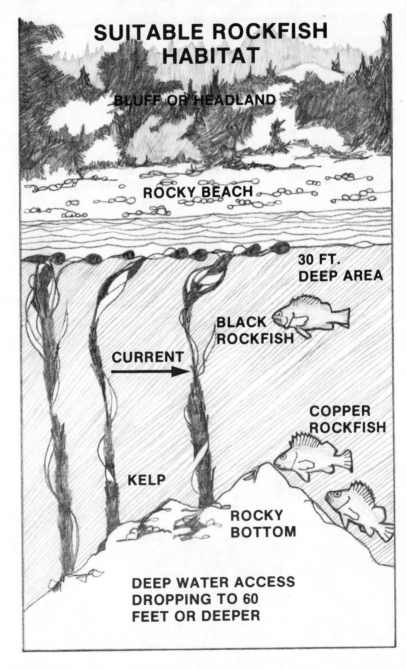

SUITABLE ROCKFISH HABITAT

BLUFF OR HEADLAND

ROCKY BEACH

30 FT. DEEP AREA

BLACK ROCKFISH

CURRENT

COPPER ROCKFISH

KELP

ROCKY BOTTOM

DEEP WATER ACCESS DROPPING TO 60 FEET OR DEEPER

3
Shallow-Water (0-40 feet) Fishing Techniques

IT IS a common misconception that the best bottom fishing is found in deep water. Our experience is exactly the opposite. Many more bottom fish species can be found at shallower depths than in deepwater, while some species never venture into deeper water. The most common species of rockfish encountered are Coppers, Browns, Quillback, Blacks, and Yellowtails. Blacks and Yellowtails are also encountered in deeper water but not necessarily on the bottom. Ling Cod and Pacific Cod venture into shallow water to feed. Other species that spend most of their lives in shallow water are Cabezon, Pile Perch, Striped Perch, Redtail Perch, Whitespotted Greenling, Kelp Greenling, Rock Sole, and Starry Flounder.

Successfully fishing shallow water for the rockfish, Pacific Cod, smaller Ling Cod, and Cabezon, can be accomplished by a variety of techniques. The long-accepted method of bottom fishing uses a mooching

Fred Vander Werff with a Copper Rockfish taken with bass casting tackle and plastic worm and jig combo.

sinker, a short leader, and herring. This rig is drifted along the bottom below the boat or dunked into openings in kelp beds. Because of the need for rebaiting and relatively little action of the bait at slow speeds, we recommend another technique. Our methods have seen little use in the Pacific Northwest, since most bottom fish have been traditionally fished for with salmon gear and herring and sought only when the salmon weren't biting. Sometimes bottom fish were taken accidentally while salmon fishing.

The new system revolves around the effectiveness of a leadhead jig and a curly-tail plastic worm. This innovative method has long been accepted on the Atlantic coast and along the southern California coast for catching salt-water species.

The most productive method for fishing with jig and worm is to first find good-looking habitat in 10 to

40 feet of water. Second, cast the jig ahead of the boat or up current and allow it to drift to the bottom. Finally, reel up the slack line and raise the rod tip to about 45 degrees, lower the rod tip to let the jig swim back to the bottom, reeling up the slack line in the process. Always maintain some tension on the line. Most strikes will occur as the jig falls back to the bottom and will only be felt if tension is maintained on the line. The strike will usually be unmistakable, but sometimes rockfish will inhale the jig with only the lightest tap. Set the hook hard on any suspicion of a fish. Don't raise the jig off the bottom too fast, or it will zoom out of the fish's field of vision before he gets a chance to strike. Also, rapid jigging will pick your jig up away from the bottom, taking it out of the strike zone. Make sure the jig touches down every time. Repeat the slow jigging motion until the lure is under the boat or the current has swept it off the bottom. Then reel in and cast again.

The secret of this method is to maintain tension on the line. Don't jig violently, and don't allow slack to develop between the rod tip and the lure. Most new-

Pile Perch

Copper Rockfish are readily available for shallow water anglers throughout Puget Sound. An average size Copper that chomped a plastic worm on a 1/2-oz. leadhead jig with bucktail dressing in Colvos Pass is landed with a thumb and forefinger grip suitable for landing most rockfish.

comers to this technique tend to overwork the jig; the slow, swimming, natural action of the jig and worm is the fish-getting system. Most of the near-shore species of bottom fish do not regularly feed on herring or fast swimming bait fish. The jig and worm does an excellent job of duplicating the action of shrimp, crabs, sculpins, and other bottom dwelling critters that these bottom fish feed on in great quantities. This method is absolutely deadly for Copper, Quillback, and Black Rockfish, Pacific Cod, Cabezon, and small Ling Cod. Fished a little deeper than 40 feet, it will get you Brown and Yellowtail Rockfish.

We discovered this productive method while fishing in the San Juan Islands of Washington. We always took along cartop boats on family camping trips to fish for trout in the lakes on these islands. As so often happens in warm summer weather, trout fishing was poor, so we dragged our boats across the beach

Cabezon are hard fighters that tear off with tenacity right up to the moment you use the gaff.

into salt water. We soon discovered our trout tackle was too light to hoist husky rockfish from the kelp beds, but we had the start of something great. Subsequent trips found us geared up to handle the situation. Our tactics were so simple and yet so productive, people at the resorts called us bald-faced liars. Our rowboats didn't give us much range, so we just rowed to the outside edge of the kelp on an incoming tide and tied the bow rope to a ball of kelp. This was years before the plastic worm was popular, so we used 1/2-ounce bucktail jigs with 4-inch pork rind trailers. Those kelp beds were loaded with hungry Copper and Quillback Rockfish. We rarely kept a legal limit until the last day of our trip, but we could easily have caught that many each time out. Every trip was spiced up by the appearance of at least one big Cabezon or Ling Cod that really tested our tackle in that underwater kelp jungle.

This is not a story of the good old days. We could launch a boat tomorrow at any location in Oregon, Washington, British Columbia, or southeast Alaska, and, weather permitting, we could catch some fish on jigs. Bear in mind good charts, a depth sounder, and a

Copper Rockfish taken on herring chunks.

seaworthy boat would insure some degree of success.

If we had time to pick our tides, investigate the area on the charts, and run the depth sounder over it, we could almost assure a full fish box. This is not an idle boast. We have already done this in areas from British Columbia's Queen Charlotte Islands to the coastal waters of Washington and Oregon. This method has never failed. Remember that careful investigation from the charts and knowledge of your target species are as important as fishing technique.

Some people balk at the idea of using artificial lures because of their cost. They also doubt their effectiveness. However, anyone who tries the jig and worm in good bottom fish areas will soon be convinced. We have taken people fishing with us that had never tried this method, and by the end of one outing they were firm believers. As for cost, consider the alternative of using bait. The mooching sinker, hooks, and leader, are not free, and the cost of frozen or fresh herring can run as high as $1.75 per dozen. Save your high-priced bait for salmon fishing and for deep water; join the fun of throwing jigs in shallow water, and you'll be pleasantly surprised at the results.

Striped Perch.

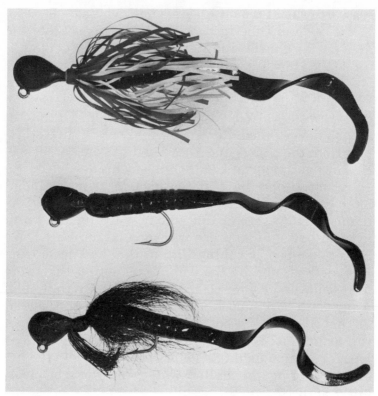

Leadhead jigs may be dressed with bucktail, left plain, or fitted with a plastic skirt, depending on an angler's preference. A nylon weed-guard, such as the one shown on the top jig, will help prevent snagging jigs in kelp and is a worthwhile addition.

JIGS AND WORMS

The weight of the jighead used depends on the amount of current and the depth of the water. For shoreline and kelp beds the 1/2-ounce size will work along the bottom and through the weeds with a minimum of snags. The round-head style with a nylon weed guard will stay out of the rocks and kelp and the fish most of the time. When fishing deeper or in heavy currents, flat-style jigs weighing 3/4 to 2 1/2 ounces will sink to the bottom and stay there. These jigs come in a variety of dressings from bare jigheads to bucktail and nylon plastic skirts, but their dressings are not as important as the plastic worm.

The curly-tail plastic worm was developed for fresh-water bass fishing but now has invaded almost every other type of fishing. The key to effectiveness of this type of plastic worm is the thin sickle-shaped tail that quivers and undulates when pulled through the water. They are manufactured in lengths from 1 1/2 inches to 9 inches. The 4-, 6-, and 7-inch lengths are most effective for the larger bottom fish. They are also made in a mind-boggling assortment of colors. We have found the darker colors most effective and tend to fish the black, purple, clear black (smoke), and dark green. Sometimes the silver, white, blue, and chartreuse colors will also be effective. We like the brands of plastic worms that are made of harder plastic than the super-soft largemouth bass worms. They are more durable under repeated attack by hard-mouthed rockfish.

Mr. Twister is the original brand of curly-tail worm and has terrific action but is a little soft. Mann's *Jelly Wiggler* and Burke's *Wig Wag* are a little more durable, and both produce that fish-getting wiggle. There are many other popular brands, and all will catch fish; these brands are mentioned so you have a name to look for when buying plastic worms. When you purchase plastic worms, buy bags of 20 or more because there is a definite savings when buying in bulk. Also, you'll need lots of worms because when you're into a bunch of marauding bottom fish, they can quickly tear and mangle a plastic worm. Save your damaged worms, as they can be repaired with a hot knife blade or a woodburner with a thin tip. You can also remelt broken pieces and mold your own plastic worms using kits available in sporting goods shops.

Other types of trailers on the jig hooks will also catch fish. One of the best to emerge recently is the new *Ripple Rind* by Uncle Josh Bait Company. This pork rind bait is shaped to produce the same action as the curly-tail plastic worm. Some of the advantages of the pork rind are its toughness and lack of buoyancy which helps the jig sink faster. Pork rind must be stored in a brine solution when not in use and cannot be allowed to dry out. However, anyone who has broken a bottle of pork rind in the bottom of a tackle box knows the inconvenience of pork rind. The spilled salt brine will quickly corrode almost every metal object in your tackle box. Packing your jar of pork rind in a sealable plastic sandwich bag may save you the mis-

Lead-body tail-spin is a highly effective lure for Black and Yellowtail Rockfishes that are surface feeding or suspended in midwater.

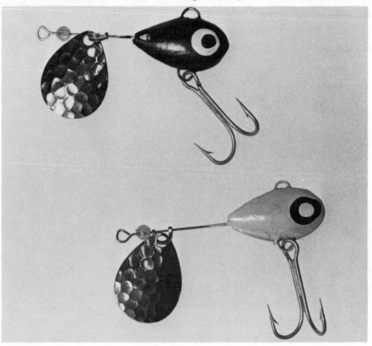

eries of a brine-saturated tackle box in the event that you might accidentally break a jar.

Another lure that works on occasion is the plain jighead and a 3-inch plastic grub. This little beaver-tailed plastic worm is very suggestive of crabs and shrimp as it bumps along the bottom. The grub is also very durable and sinks rapidly. It is made in a variety of colors but we prefer purple. The 3-inch grub is manufactured by a number of companies, but one of the best is Mann's *Sting Ray*.

Another lure that has proven itself very good for bottom fish is the lead body tail-spin. This lure resembles a lead teardrop with a spinner mounted on a shaft at the tail. The tail-spinner casts well, sinks fast, and has very attractive action. It does have a tendency to snag on anything it comes in contact with, so we clip the leading point of the treble hook. This lure is especially good for Black and Yellowtail Rockfish when they're feeding on the surface or suspended in midwater. When fishing the tail-spinner, let it sink on a tight line, because these fish hit as it falls. If you miss a strike, let the spinner fall back; sometimes they'll hit again. If no strike occurs as it falls, start retrieving just above the bottom. Let the lure drop back occasionally. It's not recommended to jig it on the bottom unless you know the bottom is not too rag-

Plain jighead with weedguard and 3-inch plastic grub.

ged. The lead tail-spinner was made famous by Tom Mann's *Little George,* a largemouth bass producer in the South made to imitate a crippled shad minnow. Other models are Pedigo's *Spinrite,* Cordell's *C.C. Shad* and, from the Puget Sound area, Luhr Jensen's *Blazer.* These tail-spinners are made in sizes from 1/4-ounce to 1 1/4-ounce. We have tried them all and all will catch fish, but most of our fishing is done with the 1/4-ounce size. While it may seem small, its compact construction allows it to cast well and sink rapidly. The color of the tail-spinner doesn't matter at all; it's the action of the lure and the way its fished that puts fish in the box.

Striped Perch are readily available to pier and shoreline bound fishermen.

When buying lures for bottom fishing, remember the abuses they will suffer in salt water. Good quality salt-water jigs must have corrosion resistant cadmium-plated or stainless-steel hooks. Bronze hooks will literally corrode overnight, making a mess in your tacklebox. If lead lures are painted, make sure they won't chip or crack easily or dissolve from contact with plastic worms. Enamel paint will be a gooey mess if stored with plastic worms. Most good quality jigs have baked epoxy finish that is impervious to the chemical action of plastic worms. If the paint on your jigs starts to dissolve, separate the worms and jigs in your tackle box. Sporting goods stores usually carry good leadheads, but if you find yourself using large quantities, it might be better to make your own. (See Chapter Seven on making your own lures.)

Using jigs effectively also requires rod, reel, and line that will handle these lures. You must be able to cast long distances with a rod that still has enough backbone to set the hook in bony jaws. The reel must be able to hold up under strain of heavy fish, and the

Small skiffs or car-toppers can increase a fisherman's ability to reach fishable spots along jetties and bays.

line must be strong enough to pull these bottom fish out of their rocky habitat. The best outfit for effectively meeting the requirements is a medium-weight steelhead rod and reel with about 12- to 17-pound test line. There are many advantages to a good baitcasting reel. A high-quality free-spool reel will handle up to 20-pound test line and permit you to cast long distances with some practice. The baitcasting reel gives you positive control over fighting fish if you clamp your thumb down on the spool. The *Ambassador 5000 D* is well suited to this purpose. Well-designed steelhead rods 7 1/2 to 8 1/2 feet long have sensitive tips, good for casting and detecting subtle bites, enough backbone to handle big fish, and long handles for forearm support. Bass casting rods function well if your wrist can hold out under the strain of casting and catching lots of fish. Bass rods have excellent casting and hook-setting characteristics, but the short handle will soon wear out all but the stoutest wrists.

Some spinning rods will work if they are not too

Ultralight gear can make the smallest rockfish seem like a lunker.

limber and the reel will handle 12- or 15-pound test line. The handle of the rod offers good support, but the spinning reel drag will slip under heavy pressure and sometimes allow big rockfish to get back into heavy cover. One way to eliminate this problem is to turn the drag all the way tight and then flip off the anti-reverse lever. Then, when hooked up to a good fish, crank him off the bottom, and, when he runs, backreel the handle and you always retain positive control. With a little practice, spinning tackle can have all the authority of a direct-drive baitcasting reel.

Ultralight tackle can be used effectively for the smaller species such as perch and greenling, but it's not recommended for the real tackle busters. Fishermen that take on big rockfish, Ling Cod and Pacific Cod, with light tackle should be experts, or they'll end up with empty tackle boxes, and a lot of fish will be swimming around with hooks and lines hanging from their mouths.

Greenling and perch are real scrappers on light tackle, and most of them will end up on the dinner table. They will readily accept baits such as pile worms, sand worms, clams, tiny crabs, and mussels. These baits fished on small hooks (sizes ranging from #8 to #2s) and light sinkers will produce lots of action.

Look along the shoreline at low tide. Dig for clams or turn over rocks to find small crabs and worms. Piers and pilings at low tide will expose enough pile worms and mussels for a day's fishing. The perch under piers can be actively feeding at any stage of the tide, but fishing from the beach or a small boat just off the beach is best done during the last stage of full tide. Flounder are real suckers for these baits when cast out and allowed to sit on the bottom. Let your bait sit for a few moments; if you don't get a bite, reel the bait a bit closer until you've retrieved your line. Cast again, working as much area as you can cover from your casting position. When looking for flounder and sole, a good fish-finding setup is a small spinner with a piece of worm dangling on a snelled hook about 12 inches behind. Drift over a muddy bay with this outfit just above the bottom until you find the flounder, then anchor and cast to the productive spot. Remember to take a long-nosed pliers or hook degouger because sometimes the bait will be swallowed.

Our preferred method of catching perch and greenling involves casting crappie jigs and retrieving them along the bottom. Crappie jigs are small lead-head jigs with a tiny plastic worm or chenille body and marabou tail on the hook. They range in size from 1/32 ounce to 1/8 ounce and come in a variety of colors. When cast with light spinning tackle and 4- to 6-pound test line, they will fish effectively. If more weight is needed, simply clamp a couple of split shot about 18 inches up the line. Greenling are very aggressive and not very choosy about types or colors of the lure. Striped Perch are much the same. Pile Perch in clear water under piers can be a problem, but they can be fooled with light line and dark-colored marabou jigs. Extracting a 3- or 4-pound perch from barnacle-encrusted pilings is a real challenge.

Our first experience with crappie jigs in salt water was while fishing for greenling in kelp beds. We traditionally thought greenling would bite only on fresh sand worms. We would spend almost half our time searching the beach for bait, only to have it nibbled off by swarms of Shiner Perch and sculpins. Also, the bait hooks frequently got snagged in the kelp. Just by chance, we found some wayward crappie jigs in the tackle box—1/8 ounce with yellow plastic worm and split tail. A light spinning rod and 6-pound test line were required to cast the small jig. To our great delight, the small jigs were gobbled up by the feeding greenling. The jig could also be manipulated around

Pile Perch are found around most piers but can be tricky to hook.

the kelp with a minimum of hang-ups. The small greenling gave us a respectable battle on the light gear. In other areas, we discovered that Striped Perch also would bite readily on the small jigs.

Pile Perch were still a problem until we tried the smaller marabou jigs. The jigs eliminated the problem of finding bait and the mess of constantly rebaiting. Also, most fish are hooked in the lip and don't require major surgery to remove the hook. You may lose a few jigs, but you gain many advantages if you fish in an area where you can cast and work the jig. The best technique for working these jigs is to cast them out and twitch them just above the bottom. Sometimes it isn't necessary to bounce the bottom on every cast. Experiment to find at what depth the perch and greenling are feeding, and work your jig at that level. You'll be surprised at the action you can stir up with this method.

Jack DeYonge works a wet-fly for rockfish off Possession Bar in central Puget Sound.

One exception to using light spinning gear for perch is when great distance casts are necessary and when fishing in the surf for Redtailed Perch. There you'll need long surf rods and 1- to 4-ounce pyramid sinkers. Usually the baited hook is tied up the line with the sinker tied on the end. The currents in the surf of coastal waters make the heavy sinkers a must.

FLY FISHING

Fly fishing for rockfish isn't a really efficient system for producing heavy catches but can provide the most fun you've ever had with a fly rod. Even with the fastest sinking fly line, practical fishing depth is limited to 20 feet or less. This leaves two types of situations for the fly rodder to fish. The first is to find Black Rockfish splashing on the surface. They're usually feeding on small shrimp or tiny herring, and this most often occurs in the dim hours of dusk or after dark. A small white bucktail fly presented on a floating or sink-tip line will get all the action you can handle. The beauty of this situation is the lack of snags, so you can play your fish to your heart's content. On a fly rod, the strength of the fish is magnified, and big Blacks can run and run. If these fish were jumpers, we're sure they would have a bigger following among fly fishermen. Any fly rodder who is looking for some fast action on a warm summer evening should try fishing for Black Rockfish.

The second occasion for a fly fisherman to get his line stretched is to be in a kelp bed for the last couple hours in a flood tide. If this occurs in the late afternoon or evening, it can be really fast and furious. You'll find mostly Copper Rockfish, so getting down to the bottom is a must. The best line for this is a high density shooting head, although a full sinking line will work too. The obstructions are many, so careful casting and weedless flies will help to keep hang-ups to a minimum. Some of the best flies for fishing in the kelp are Dave Whitlock's bottom crawling bass flies tied on stainless-steel hooks with a looped nylon weed guard. These flies were designed to be the fly fisherman's an-

Flyrodder Jack DeYonge lands a small Copper Rockfish that grabbed his sinking fly off Possession Bar in central Puget Sound.

swer to the plastic worm. The drab, buggy-looking creations are well suited to working in heavy cover. Other flies that work well are the marabou blossom series. The marabou is fragile but it has terrific action. If you tie your own flies, here is the opportunity to dream up your own killer patterns because no one has really investigated the possibilities.

Fly rods for rockfish should have long, powerful shafts capable of pushing a weight forward or shooting head 9-weight line and a 3/0 fly against a saltwater breeze for long casts. The long rod is also useful for pulling hefty rockfish out of masses of kelp. Anglers set up for winter steelhead fly fishing already have all the necessary equipment. One useful tip for fishing sinking lines and big flies is to use short, heavy leaders. The stiff leader helps turn over the big fly, and keeping it short will help the fly to sink deep with the line.

After you've mastered the technique of catching lots of bottom fish and you're looking for added thrills, try the fly rod. You won't be disappointed.

FLY ROD AND HERRING

For anglers that may want to try the thrill of playing rockfish on a fly rod but would prefer using bait, here's the method which we've used in Puget Sound for catching rockfish with fly rods and herring.

Fly rods and herring used at the edge of a kelp bed on the beginning of an incoming tide can provide the kind of action from shallow-water rockfishes that will leave your wrist aching and your fish box amply filled with the makings for dinner. It's an excellent method to use from rocky shorelines, breakwaters, and jetties, or from a small cartopper boat. Fly rod and herring require little investment in tackle and frequently offer close-to-home fishing.

All you'll need is a fly rod, preferably rigged with sinking fly line, a few salmon-style mooching leaders, large split shot and a small supply of herring. A dozen herring should be adequate for a single angler to catch a satisfactory supply of Coppers and in some locations, Black Rockfish.

Time your arrival to the tail end of an outgoing tide, selecting a place where you can cast into a spot of open water in the kelp, ideally the tip of a breakwater or point of land if you're shorebound.

When the tide starts to turn and rise, cast a whole herring hooked with the standard double-hook setup, weighted with a single buckshot-sized splitshot sinker about 2 feet above the hooks into an open spot in the kelp. It should have time to sink several feet before drifting back into the kelp with the gentle tidal flow. Your bait will flutter gently through the kelp as you feed line out; generally not more than 20 or 30 feet of line should be fed out before you wait for a strike.

Rockfish taking the bait presented in this manner with fly tackle will normally swim up from their resting place in the kelp bed, inhale the herring, and turn back for the rock crevice where they generally lie in wait for unwary prey.

Instead of a light nibble or hard strike, the signal to set the hook is the steady pull that is suddenly exerted on your rod tip as the fish moves off with the bait in its mouth. Frequently your line will start moving off, and the rod tip will be pulled right to the water as the fish moves off. Set the hook at this movement! Make sure you're well balanced, as you'll be surprised at the power of the initial run of a 2- or 3-pound rockfish hooked on fly tackle. It takes strong pressure to stop the fish's surge for the safety of the kelp and rocks when it feels the hook.

Hand strip your line back as quickly as you can, as you turn the fish and work it out from the forest of kelp to where you can play it in open water. You won't have time to reel the fish in most cases and will have to use the hand-stripping technique until you can hold the fish in open water. Here you'll have time to reel in your slack, while holding the fish on a tight line.

Once you land your fish, stun, and bleed it and sling another herring into the same slot. The action is usually fast in this type of light-tackle fishing, and you will normally take as many fish as you can rea-

Rocky northern California coastline offers a variety of rockfish, sculpins, and perch.

Perch are frequent catches for the shore-bound fisherman casting from rocky or sandy shoreline.

sonably use in the first hour of the tide's turning, *if your wrist holds out that long!*

JETTY AND ROCK FISHING

From a practical standpoint, most salt-water fishing is done by boat because it allows greater mobility and access to more areas than are available to the shorebound angler. But, fishing from shorelines and jetties should not be overlooked. Rock and jetty fishing have a charm and frustration all their own.

For the shorebound angler, it offers the opportunity to catch nearly all of the shallow-water rockfishes, flatfish, sculpins, and greenling with an occasional Ling Cod under lucky circumstances.

Without a doubt, the greatest hazard in rock and jetty fishing is the tackle-grabbing appetite of the environment where you'll be casting. Since you'll be casting out over the edge of rocks and kelp or right in the midst of them, you can't help but lose lots of terminal tackle. On the other hand, you don't have to have a lot of expensive equipment to get out and catch a dinner or two of rockfish.

A rather long rod of medium to heavy caliber is preferred, primarily to allow you to reach over the kelp or place your jig or bait in an opening in the kelp alongside the rocks. A standard medium star drag reel or spinning reel works best with these rods. You can use shorter boat rods, as well as medium weight rigs like steelhead drift rods or salmon mooching rods, but they lack the backbone to pull a snagged jig or terminal tackle free. Larger rods may give you a better chance at retrieving your terminal gear without losing the entire rig.

If you can locate a spot on a jetty where you can get your line through an opening in the kelp and down

Walleye Surfperch taken on spinning tackle from LaPush, Washington breakwater.

to a depth of 10 or 15 feet and work with a straight line down from the rod tip, jigging with plastic worms or feather jigs can be super!

If you're having to cast out over the rocks to reach the fish, it may be better to fish bait, as the cost of losing a dozen or so jigs will be enough to spoil anyone's day.

Thirty-pound test monofilament is about the right weight for general rock and jetty fishing. It's not too heavy to cast, but strong enough to pull free when hung up in the kelp or rocks in many cases.

Many rock and jetty fishermen save themselves a bundle in the cost of sinkers by using spark plugs or sand filled *Bull Durham* sacks. If you can get your local service station to save you a can full of spark plugs as they replace them on tuneups, you'll soon have enough weights to handle any of your rock and jetty fishing outings. The best way to rig these is to tie an overhand knot in the end of your leader which can be slipped through the gap of the spark plug; close the gap by pounding it on a rock and place your hooks, usually two on short leaders with one about a foot above the sinker and the second a foot higher than the bottom hook leader. You may want to use slightly lighter test leaders than the main line so if you do snag and have to break off you'll lose only the hook.

Clams, mussels, bits of herring, or tube or sand worms are all good bait for rock and jetty fishing.

Trying jetties or rocky shorelines in your area will let you determine the best time to fish as far as tide conditions go. Generally, high tide seems to be the best time for this type of bottom fishing, as the fish are moving in closer to feed and appear to be more active on a high or incoming tide.

If you have a small cartopper or skiff that can be hand launched around a jetty, they can provide you with much greater access. You can work right at the edge of the kelp line or tie up in the middle of the kelp and fish directly down, which will eliminate hanging up tackle as frequently as casting from the shore. Small boats should only be used around jetties where the area is well protected and the water is flat.

If you're planning to fish a jetty on the open ocean such as the mouths of most ports along the coastline, never use a small boat except on very calm days and only on the inside of the jetty. Never—absolutely never—fish from a small boat around jetties on the open ocean! A large wave at the wrong moment can be extremely dangerous. Where you're fishing from a rocky shoreline or jetty and there is considerable wave action, extreme caution is advised, as this can be very unsafe. Never place yourself in the possible situation of being caught unexpectedly by a large wave which will easily sweep you off your feet. Common sense in safety is the keyword to jetty and rocky shoreline fishing.

Nighttime fishing from shorelines, jetties, and piers is a sport that offers new challenges for bottom fishermen. Black Rockfish which can be very scarce around jetties and piers during most of the daylight hours tend to become aggressive feeders towards evening and frequently move in around the edges of piers and jetties to feed right on or near the surface.

Fishing with light spinning tackle and jigs with plastic worms or fly rods and white streamer flies can get hot and heavy when a school of Blacks moves into casting range as darkness approaches. If you're fishing from a lighted pier or breakwater, the action can continue long after dark.

Fred Vander Werff lands a Pacific Cod in central Puget Sound.

Pacific Cod

4
Medium-Depth (40-200 feet) Fishing Techniques

MEDIUM-WATER-depth bottom fishing in the 40- to 200-foot range requires some adjustments in tactics, equipment, and techniques. You may also find some of the deep-water bottom fishes in the deep end of the midwater scale, as well as many of those species found in shallow waters.

Joining the Copper Rockfish and the two species of rockfish that tend to move up and down in the water column, Black and Yellowtail Rockfish, you can expect to find heavy concentrations of Pacific Cod, Pollack, and some of the tackle-busting bottom fish—Ling Cod, Yelloweye Rockfish, Canary Rockfish, Boccacio, and Halibut. Yelloweye Rockfish are commonly referred to by most anglers as Red Snapper. This is a misnomer, as there are actually no true species of Red Snapper on the North Pacific coast. Quillbacks, Brown Rockfish, and, on the outer coastline of Washington and waters of British Columbia, China Rock-

57

Walleye Pollack

fish are found in medium-depth ranges. Cabezon, various sole and flounders, and Halibut are found at these depths as well.

The medium-water depths are the best sportfishing areas for Ling Cod from 40 feet on down, with their relative, the greenling, being taken in the depths from the shallow-water zone to 150 feet.

PACIFIC COD

In Puget Sound, fall through spring fishing for Pacific Cod, Pollack, and Tom Cod is exceptionally good, particularly when the Pacific Cod start showing up in massive schools for spawning.

Pacific Cod are found in heavy concentrations in the Strait of Juan de Fuca, Bellingham Bay, Agate Passage, Fox Island, Point Fosdick, and the Point Defiance areas of south Puget Sound during fall through early spring.

Typically stormy weather through the winter and spring, restricts the average sport fisherman from fishing for cod in the Strait of Juan de Fuca. On less windy days, many of the Puget Sound locations offer exceptional fishing for Pacific Cod and Pollack, generally in 60 to 150 feet of water or more.

The most popular bait for cod is herring, preferably live, hooked with a 2-hook-tie salmon rig and used with weight sufficient to reach bottom in normal tide flow and wind action. You may need from 2 to 16 ounces of lead. Heavier weights will get you down to the fish when the 16-ounce leads won't hold bottom. However, under these severe conditions resulting from too much wind or tidal current, your best bet is to haul in your lines and move into shallower and more protected waters where you can turn to shallow-water techniques.

When fishing herring for bottom fish such as cod and Pollack, a shorter leader is required than the

Doug Wilson with a good-sized Pacific Cod that inhaled a herring fished in a shallow water kelp bed in Puget Sound.

standard 6-foot salmon mooching leader. A 2-foot leader is ideal. Many anglers prefer live herring, and, when fishing bait, this would be our first choice. Herring can be kept live in a container where the water is aerated or frequently changed. A 10-gallon plastic bucket or medium-sized ice chest with frequent water changes will keep up to 4 dozen herring fairly healthy for several hours.

When fishing frozen or fresh dead herring, we prefer to fish cut plug herring rather than the whole fish. Cut plugs are much more effective in drawing strikes as they have more spin than whole-rigged herring when gently raised from the bottom.

Hooked live bait will provide the action to attract these bottom feeders as you drift through an area. A dead bait just drags along behind your sinker with relatively little action. Obviously, there are times when you can just plunk it to the bottom and a fish will oblige by striking. Your catch and strike ratio will be greatly enhanced, however, by using the following techniques when fishing herring.

Spool your bait and sinker to the bottom, let it bounce on the bottom, then slowly raise your rod tip from near water level to nearly straight above your head, drop the rod tip again, making sure that the sinker bangs the bottom. Gently raise the rod tip again. The sound vibrations created by the sinker banging the bottom will draw the attention of fish in the area, and they will follow the sound to investigate. Gently raising your rod tip pulls the bait from the bottom giving it a spinning action that will entice a strike, which you may feel as a mere nibble as the fish mouths the bait. Gently lower the rod tip a couple of feet when you feel that gentle bite—more than the sinker weight on the business end of your line.

Frequently a bottom fish will mouth, spit out a bait, then pick it up again. This makes it extremely important that you know the fish is still mouthing the bait when you set the hook. If the fish starts to move off with the bait, you'll feel a strong steady pull that will take your rod tip downward. Frequently, this movement will be punctuated by several sharp taps.

Set the hook firmly but gently. Cod have delicate mouths and the hook can easily be torn free by an overly eager angler using too much snap when setting the hook or reefing to hard when pumping the fish from the bottom.

Knowing the power of your tackle is important in both setting the hook and playing the fish. Light- to medium-weight rods such as standard steelhead or salmon mooching rods are much more forgiving than a stiff boat rod. Tidal flow and wind permitting, the best sport comes with using light tackle.

In near slack water conditions, a standard 7 1/2- to 8 1/2-foot steelhead rod and level-wind reel will provide you with the tools to hook fish in depths to 150 feet. Rods of this caliber can seldom handle more than 3 or 4 ounces of lead, but if you pick your tides and weather, you'll get great enjoyment from using this tackle. You will be surprised how often you'll feel fish that you would be completely unaware of when using sturdier gear.

The greatest joy of all is discovering that the Pacific Cod or Pollack that felt like a waterlogged rubber boot on heavier tackle affords a challenging fight and will not come up so easily on lighter gear. A 7- or 8-pound Pacific Cod hauled from the depths of 100 or more feet can still run and strip line with unexpected energy as he nears the boat when played on light tackle.

When you get your fish on the surface, a deft stroke with a hand gaff through the fish's head, so as not to damage the fillets, is the easiest way to bring the fish aboard. Wear rubber work gloves to remove the hook and handle your catch. Gloves prevent nicks and cuts which will be irritated further by salt water. Cuts may not hurt when you're excited and catching fish, but you'll be surprised how painful these little cuts can be the following day.

Cod flesh goes soft quickly. For the best quality filets, bleed the fish immediately and put it on ice. This is really a prerequisite for handling your catch of any fish if you want the finest quality for the table.

Get your bait into the strike zone as quickly as you can after dispatching your fish. Repeat the bottom banging process with the sinker. Try to keep the bait in the strike zone, which is basically from a few inches off the bottom up to 4 or 5 feet for Pacific Cod and frequently higher for Pollack. At times Pollack may school further off the bottom or follow a bait several feet on the retrieve before picking it up.

You'll frequently catch Tom Cod, a much smaller but very tasty cod, while fishing for Pacific Cod and Pollack. Although not heavily fished, Hake are excellent food fish that require immediate icing, as they go soft quickly. Hake are most commonly caught with herring just before daylight and in the late evening.

Many anglers prefer to fish for cod and Pollack with jigs, since it's equally, if not more, efficient,

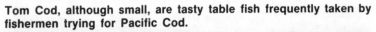

Tom Cod, although small, are tasty table fish frequently taken by fishermen trying for Pacific Cod.

eliminates the mess of handling bait, and unless you lose a lot of jigs entails less expense than buying 3 or 4 dozen herring for an outing. Nordic jigs in the 3- to 4-ounce size can be used with medium tackle. Our odds on favorite for steelhead-weight tackle, however, is the plastic worm fished in the following ways.

Up to about 130 feet of water, leadhead jigs such as the Hopkins *Hammertail* in 2 1/2-ounce weight rigged with a black or purple 6- or 9-inch curly-tailed plastic worm are our first choice. Some anglers prefer to use a standard 3- or 4-ounce mooching sinker with a long shanked hook attached directly to a sinker swivel and a 9-inch plastic worm. Heavier crescent sinkers rigged in this manner will allow you to fish the sinker, plastic-worm jig on the bottom when a couple of ounces won't hold in the current and may be fished deeper than the *Hammertail* jigs.

A third method for rigging plastic worms that provides constant action uses a mooching sinker on the main line, a 2-foot leader tied to the sinker, and a

Deeper than the 40-foot level, heavier jigs are required to reach the bottom. One of the best leadheads available in the 1 1/2- to 2 1/2- ounce size is *Hopkins* stainless steel *Hammertail* rigged with a plastic worm.

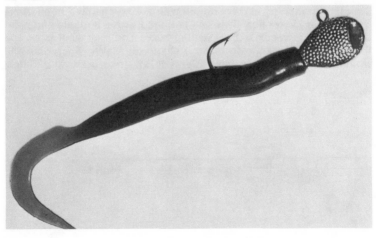

rubber worm with a large "Little Corky" steelhead bobber rigged on the leader just in front of the hook-rigged worm. To keep the bobber from sliding up the leader, tie a piece of thread with a couple of overhead knots on the leader and snug it down on the topside of the bobber or pin it with a toothpick. You may want to try substituting a hoochie on this third method. However, our feelings are that the plastic worm is superior for drawing strikes.

A combination of the worm and hoochie is another variation worth trying. Hopkins *NO-EQL* jigging spoons and *Stingsilda* are excellent jigs for deeper fishing during light tidal flow. Nordic jigs, ranging from 4 ounces up to 17 1/2 ounces are excellent producers on all bottom fish. Their one great disadvantage is cost. Some of the better nordic jigs—slightly fluted long silver jigs rigged with a treble hook—retail as high as $7, which is enough to make an angler cry when he loses one of these larger jigs. When using these very heavy jigs, use stouter rods and 60- to 80-pound test *Dacron* line. In many instances you can pull a jig hooked on the bottom free from a snaggy bottom if this heavy *Dacron* line is used. Another ad-

Standard mooching sinkers rigged with a long-shanked hook make good deeper water jigs. This one is rigged with a hoochie and plastic worm on a weedless bass fishing hook. You may want to scrape the sinker with a knife to make it shinier; however, it is debatable whether a shine makes any difference in strike drawing abilities.

vantage to *Dacron* is that it has little stretch, making it preferable to monofilament for jigging in the deeper depths of the mid-zone and into the deep-water zone.

Somewhat less expensive but excellent heavy jigs are pipe jigs, which are easily made at home from copper plumbing tubing or aluminum tubing filled with lead. Details for making these jigs are covered in Chapter Seven on making your own salt-water jigs.

Straight vertical jigging will frequently produce fish. Results seem to be more impressive, however, if the jig is fished at an angle to the boat. During slack tides it's best to cast your jig away from the boat and let it sink to the bottom, making sure that you've free-spooled plenty of line so that the jig will reach bottom several feet away from the boat. On a running tide or if your boat is being pushed by a light breeze, you can drop the jig straight down, then free-spool additional line to position it at an angle from the boat before jigging. Gently arch the rod to raise the jig from the bottom, then let it flutter back to bounce on the bottom again. Keeping your jig at an angle to the boat is the key to working it over as much bottom as possible each time you cast. It is very important that the jigging motion be slow enough to just raise the lure a few feet off the bottom, then let it flutter back down.

Nordic Jigs ranging up to 17 1/2 ounces are standard deepwater jigs balanced to heavy rod and reel and heavy test Dacron line.

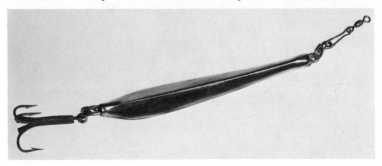

Most bottom fish are not able to pursue a moving lure quickly, whereas a slow-moving fluttering lure gives the fish a chance to take a swipe at it. If you retrieve your jig with a rapid motion, you'll be pulling it away from many fish that would otherwise have time to clamp down on it. Many times a fish will pick up the lure as it flutters back down. You can actually feel the fish moving off with the jig in its mouth much like the telegraph of a bite from a fish picking up a bait.

Homemade pipe jigs are popular for deepwater jigging.

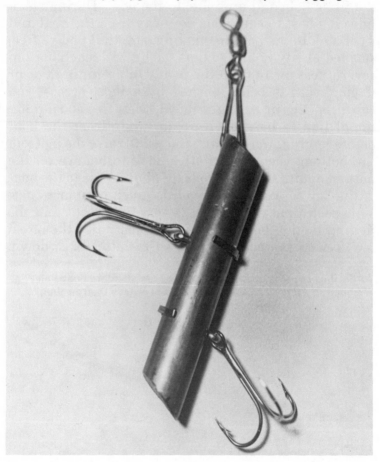

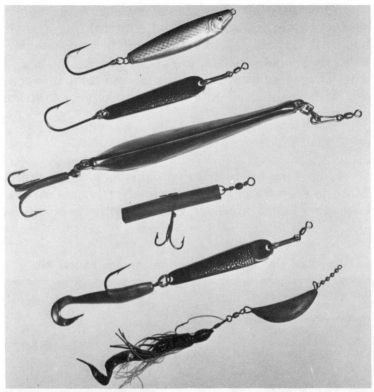

Mid-depth to deepwater jigs are from the top: Norwegian made *Stingsilda, Hopkins NO-EQL, Nordic Pilks,* homemade pipejigs, *Hopkins Swimming Tail NO-EQL,* and a mooching sinker rigged with *Hoochie* and plastic worm.

With these larger jigs, if a fish gets the hooks in his mouth, you'll nearly always have him hooked solidly, due to the large hook size and the weight of the lure falling with a slack line. When you get a bump on the jig but don't hook the fish, let it drop to the bottom immediately and gently pull it up with a full jigging arch. In 90 percent of these instances you'll have an instant hookup from the fish that just bumped the lure the first time around. When fishing in schools of Pacific Cod or Pollack with these larger jigs, it is quite common to foul hook a fish.

Since fish hear low frequency sound through a sensory organ running along the lateral line of their bodies, it is quite possible that some fish hooked, particularly schooling ones, are zeroing in on the sound activity created by working the jig and come into contact with the hooks before they have a chance to strike the lure.

LING COD

Ling Cod are generally considered a medium-depth to deep-water fish in Pacific Northcoast waters. Like other fishes, however, there can always be the ex-

Ling Cod are one of the most sought after bottom fish.

ception, as we've caught Lings in 15 to 30 feet in Washington and Oregon year around.

Lings move into fairly shallow water during the winter to spawn and are frequently taken in the shallow-water zone. Other than winter fishing, Lings are generally going to be commonly caught from the beginning of the mid-depth zone all the way to deep water where you'll need specialized tackle to fish for them. Lings are one of the more popularly sought bottom fish because of their size and especially for their quality as a food fish.

Beginning at the edge of the medium-water zone on to deeper depths, there are definite methods that will put more Lings on the business end of your line.

Medium-weight tackle, such as steelheading rods or light mooching rods, used along the edges of kelp beds will give you the best sport for Ling Cod of average size. Lings generally average 9 to 12 pounds where you're angling for a variety of bottom fish in the shallow end of the medium-water depths. Lings tend to be larger as you fish deeper. Since they reach weights in excess of 70 pounds, if you do accidentally hook one of these monsters in shallower water on your mooching gear, your chances of landing him are remote. You'll end up sitting in your boat with a dazed expression muttering and speculating on what it was that took your bait and nearly tore the rod from your hands as line sizzled through the guides. All your efforts with drag and thumb pressure were to no avail, ending up with you breaking off a badly frayed line. Mr. Lunker Ling has merely run back to the safety of an underwater cave or crevice and you've just lost the battle!

Matched with the right tackle, you might have had a chance, but losing one like this is what makes for "fish stories." On the more practical side, the smaller Lings usually caught along the kelp beds can

Pump a Ling Cod up slowly, then be prepared for at least one line stripping run when he nears the boat.

be tough customers on your mooching gear. They will give you all the tussle you can handle with this tackle.

Trolling a whole herring right along the edge of the kelp at very slow speeds with the bait only a foot or two off the bottom will frequently produce Lings. Make sure that you're trolling slowly enough that the bait is making a slow roll as it's trolled behind a 2- or 3-ounce crescent sinker on about a 3-foot leader rigged with 2/0 to 3/0 hooks.

Being the toothy creatures that Lings are, they can and will rough up your leaders, so it's usually a good idea to use a fairly heavy leader—20- to 30-pound test. Such a leader will probably be heavier test than your main line in this case. When you do snag up, expect to lose your complete terminal rig.

Here's a handy trick for protecting your leaders when fishing for Lings, which also saves many a leader if you find yourself fishing where you're getting Dogfish, the salmon angler's nonfavorite herring chomper. Use clear plastic tubing (the type used for insulation of wire in electrical equipment) that is just large enough to thread your leader through and slip over the eye and knot of the hook. Intravenous feeding tubing from hospital supply firms is basically the same type of material. Either of these types of tubing will do the job. It just depends on where it is easiest for you to purchase it.

Tie you own double hook salmon-type mooching leaders, using 2 to 3 inches of tubing slipped over the bottom hook's leader. Repeat the process with the second hook. By saving lots of time changing leaders, you gain more time with your line in the water.

Lings, when hooked in shallower water, may come towards the surface with little difficulty as you gently

Unless you're skilled with a hand gaff, larger bottom fish such as Ling Cod are best handled with a net.

pump them up, *until they see the shadow of the boat!!!*
Suddenly that pulsating log on the other end of your
line will decide he isn't going to come up into the sun-
light.

Watch your thumb! If you fish with a lightly set
drag, as preferred by most experienced fishermen,
your thumb will get a workout. If you're not expecting
the line-ripping run that a Ling is capable of, you'll
end up with a burned thumb from the speed of the line
stripping from the reel. A lightly set drag and an
educated thumb are much preferred for handling any

**For big Ling Cod, the best bait is a live Greenling from 1 to 2 pounds,
rigged with large hooks and fished right off the bottom.**

fish you'll catch in Northwest salt waters. If you have set your drag too tightly, the sudden run of a Ling will virtually take your rod away from you, pulling it down so sharply that it will whack the gunwale of your boat. Unless you can lighten the drag quickly during one of these power-charged runs, the fish will most likely break off in his dash for the safety of bottom rocks and crevices.

As you play a Ling on light tackle he will probably give you three or four of these line-sizzling runs before you can bring him alongside the boat. Use a salmon net, or, if you're skilled with one, a good sturdy gaff. Unless you've gaffed a lot of fish, we suggest using a salmon net for bringing your catch aboard. Stun your fish before attempting to remove the hook, and then be sure to use a pair of pliers or a hook remover and heavy work gloves if you value your fingers. Ling Cod have teeth that will inflict a very painful incision if you're careless. Almost equally hazardous are the Ling's gills.

Besides trolling the edge of kelp beds, another excellent location to look for Ling Cod in the shallow end of mid-depth waters is by working around offshore rocks along the coastline. In most areas, tidal flow is not a factor to be concerned with in open ocean fishing, as opposed to areas like Puget Sound and waters going north through British Columbia and southeast Alaska's island-strewn coastline. The greatest safety concern in fishing around offshore rocks is wave action and ground swells. Never fish in areas where waves or swells are breaking without keeping your boat motor running at all times as a safety factor. The motor may save you and your boat if you suddenly find yourself picked up by a swell and headed for the rocks. Good common sense is the rule here.

Work around the rocks by dropping your lines to the bottom, then picking them up about a half dozen

Ling cod don't come to the boat easily, Don Dudley is ready with the gaff as Fred Vander Werff plays a big Ling hooked with a live Greenling on the Washington Coast.

turns of the reel. Motor slowly along the edge of the rocks, occasionally throwing the motor into neutral then back into gear, giving your bait a fluttering motion as you pick up slack in moving the boat. This will entice any fish waiting for a meal to pass by.

Jigging spoons and leadhead jigs work well in these spots but you'll have to expect frequent hang-ups. The cost of lost tackle may sway your choice to the use of bait, either herring, smelt, candlefish, or squid. Squid can be bought frozen in 5-pound boxes from many fish shops and make an excellent bait for nearly all bottom fish. Squid are much tougher and stay on the hook far better than herring, which saves constant rebaiting.

Ling Cod are very aggressive feeders and are frequently caught by anglers who are playing a smaller bottom fish. Suddenly the rod slams down in a solid and ungiving arc like a freight train suddenly came along and snagged the line in passing.

Play this fish gently! In most cases he will be just holding onto the small hooked fish. Unless a dangling loose hook lodges in the Ling's cavernous maw, he may look you right in the eye when you get him to the boat and spit out a 2- or 3-pound rockfish, then slowly sink from sight as you stand there shaking.

Being so aggressive by nature, Ling Cod apparently will home in on a disturbance of a thrashing fish from some distance and come zeroing in to grab the smaller fish you're playing in shallower waters.

If you are particularly after big Lings, the most successful method we know is to catch a few Kelp

All mouth and teeth—Fred's 20-pound Ling with the 2-pound bait in its mouth.

Greenling, small rockfish, or sole in the shallows. Place them in a large bucket or garbage can filled with enough salt water to keep them healthy. Aerate the water frequently by exchanging it with fresh scoops of salt water to keep up the oxygen content, or use a small battery-operated aerator. Once you've caught enough bait, move off to deeper water over a known rocky bottom or reef and get ready for muscle strain.

Hook your live bait through the upper lip with the lead hook, then thread your second hook just under the skin of the upper back and out so it will dangle alongside the bait's back. Use heavy leaders (30- to 60-pound test) and very large hooks (7/0 to 9/0) so there is still point and barb exposed after hooking the bait. A 4- to 6-ounce sinker with about a 3-foot leader works well, as you can tell for sure when you've reached the bottom by the sinker bounce. Reel up about 4 or 5 feet of line so that the bait will be swimming just far enough off the bottom that he can't lodge himself in a crevice in the rocks. He will be exposed to the view of any Ling lying in wait as you drift over him.

When the rod tip dips in a steady arc, pulling the tip beneath the surface, gently feed a bit of slack, then tighten the line slightly and wait for the next steady pull as the Ling swims off. Set the hook as hard as you can; don't worry about pulling the bait out of his mouth. You must pull the hooks out of the greenling and into the Ling Cod's tough mouth, as he may be just holding onto your bait with his mouth closed. If you miss the Ling Cod on the first strike, free-spool your bait back to bottom, and frequently he'll grab it again. When you feel the second grab, wait for the strong pull and set the hook. Work him up slowly and gently by steady pumping. It may take several minutes to work up a large Ling from over 100 feet.

Lings, once they are pulled off the bottom and unless they are rising to the surface somewhat of their

Fred holds the bait and his 12-pound prize. The same bait caught a 20-pounder earlier.

own volition, will frequently open their mouths wide. You'll find your self pumping up a huge fish with his mouth wide open, which is like trying to haul up a bucket full of water from a great depth. Besides being muscle-rending work, the sight of that huge maw coming into view as you raise the fish from the darkness of deeper water will likely be a bit of a shock to your nervous system.

If your Ling is apparently only holding onto your bait fish, he will likely rise towards the surface under steady pumping, steadfastly holding onto the bait. He will not make any hard runs since he doesn't seem to be aware that he is being played in. As far as he seems to be concerned he is interested only in keeping a good grip on the fish he has grabbed, and he isn't about to let go. Remember, don't pull his head out of the water when attempting to land him, or he'll thrash around and get away.

During a fishing trip on the Washington coast off Cape Flattery one summer, we were taking large Quillback Rockfish in about 120 feet in the 5-pound class while fishing about a mile offshore on a calm, flat day.

The first Quillback that came up was being closely followed by a shadow about 3 1/2 feet long. As the two fish came into clearer view at about 30 feet, there was a large Ling, about 30 pounds, slowly rising with the hooked Quillback and circling it without attempting to grab it. Since a large Quillback represents a lot of sharp spines, a Ling will not readily grab one of these rockfish. If it does, normally it will be from the tail end and behind the dorsal fin. About 10 feet from the surface the Ling turned lazily and sank into the depths as we boated the Quillback. Two more Quillback came up in subsequent minutes with Lings of similar size circling them but shying off even though we stopped playing the hooked Quillback at about 30 feet, hoping the Ling would pick it off.

The next fish to pick up one of our large herring baits was a medium Ling about 12 pounds. As it came into sight, a huge shadow loomed alongside it. We were so nervous, we spoke in whispers when we spotted the shadow. We stopped reeling and waited to see if the large Ling would take the smaller one. The movement of the line was stopped. The big Ling grabbed the smaller one, and we could see it with only a third of the fish sticking out of the big Ling's mouth. The larger fish let go, spitting out his 12-pound morsel, then grabbed it again and hung on as we slowly worked in the line. At about 20 feet he let go of the smaller Ling, which he had nearly inhaled, circled and grabbed it by the side of the head, clamping down with a determined grip. The big Ling was slowly pumped, and, as it lay on the surface with the smaller Ling

Quillback Rockfish make a spiny mouthful for Ling Cod; however, on occasion a rockfish like this will become the bait for big fish after he chomps a herring or jig.

firmly in its grip, we gently slid our salmon net under them and came up with a quick thrust, netting both the large unhooked Ling and his intended prey in a single motion. We reared back attempting to swing the fish aboard, only to discover that they couldn't be raised from the water with the net in the normal manner. We had to quickly grab the other side of the net and hoist aboard by holding the net frame with both hands. Rapping both fish with our stunning club, we got out the scales. Our bait, which had inhaled an 8-inch herring bait, ran 12 pounds. The cannibalistic Ling that tried to take the 12-pounder for dinner weighed 42 1/2 pounds. After this episode that put 54 1/2 pounds of Ling Cod in the boat in 10 suspense-filled minutes, a 24-pound Ling plus a couple 10- to 20-

Rockfish like this 10-pound Yellow Eye held by Doug Wilson have large mouths. When fishing with bait, wait until the fish is moving off and exerting a strong downward pull on the rodtip, then set the hook firmly. If the fish is just mouthing the bait, you can jerk the hook right out of his mouth when trying to set it.

pound Yelloweye Rockfish that came after seemed anticlimactic!

Big Lings, like the 42 1/2-pounder, can come in very easily, since they come nearly to the surface on their own before ending up in the net. A large Ling, hooked at depth and aware that he is somehow in trouble, may require 30 or 40 minutes of careful handling to bring up from 100 to 150 feet.

Many fishermen get over-anxious, pump too hard, and break off these monster Lings. With careful handling and patience we've hauled Lings weighing 65 and 57 pounds from waters off Neah Bay on a single weekend on standard medium-heavy-weight salt-water rods and 30-pound test monofilament.

You don't need broomstick poles with winching power reels to land big Lings. The primary reason for using these extra heavy pieces of tackle rigged with wire line is for their ability to handle the heft of the heavy leads you'll need to fish at great depth, rather than being able to work the fish up.

DEEP-WATER ROCKFISH

Deep-water rockfish—Yelloweye, Canary, and Boccacio—begin to show up at the deeper end of medium-depth range. Normally associated with waters around 200 feet deep and deeper, Yelloweye begin to appear in catches at about 130 to 150 feet. They are usually much deeper in Puget Sound but are found at the shallower depths on the ocean coastline and waters north of the Canadian border. Use of good charts and a depth sounder are almost imperative for successful and consistent catches of these deep water dwelling rockfishes. Charted areas known to produce will guide you in finding these fish; use of a sounder will greatly increase your effectiveness to the point of astounding you.

In areas with strong current flow from tidal action, such as Puget Sound, the San Juan Islands, and the inside salt-water areas of British Columbia and Alaska, reaching these fish is restricted to periods of slow tidal movement at the peak of high tide or at slack ebb. Those periods are frequently limited to only a few minutes in some areas. Spots that can only be fished when the current is just right can be a jackpot of action for under 30 minutes and then become completely unfishable, even with the special gear covered in Chapter Five on deep water fishing.

In coastal waters tide fluctuation is not such a determining factor. You can reach deep water species at the upper end of their depth range with as little as 4 to 8 ounces of lead or jigs in the same weight class. The water must be calm, and wind must not be pushing your boat along at too fast a clip.

Large herring or squid have been our preferred baits at these depths. Big fish have big mouths and can gulp down a large herring easily. Squid, bought in 5-pound boxes (frozen) from fish dealers, make a tougher bait that will stay on the hook better than herring. Frequently squid generate a quick response from feeding rockfish. Take both along if possible.

Nordic jigs, pipe jigs, and in really calm or slack waters, jigging spoons provide solid hookups without the mess of bait. The jigging spoons should be bounced along the bottom at a slight angle to the boat to give them a fluttering action as they are jigged off the bottom and allowed to sink again. Jigs and spoons mean more work for the fisherman who must constantly work his jig to draw strikes. Using both jigs and bait in medium depth provides varied results on different outings. Be prepared to fish with both.

Don Dudley with a good-sized Yellow Eye Rockfish taken off Cape Flattery in 140 feet of water.

Bait can be fished with medium-weight salt-water rods and level wind reels loaded with 30-pound test monofilament. Jigging can be done with the same rod and reel combination; however, we highly recommend using a stiffer rod and changing to *Dacron* line for jigging. *Dacron* line in the 60- to 80-pound test weight is suggested for jigging beyond depths of 100 feet to a couple hundred feet. At those depths you'll likely be using heavier jigs, such as the large nordics or pipe jigs that weight up to a pound or more.

You won't need that heavy a line to land any fish you're liable to hook unless a barn door Halibut sucks up your jig. You'll discover the necessity of the heavy *Dacron* line the first time your jig hangs up on bottom. Losing a commercial nordic jig that cost as much as 3 or 4 dozen herring is a painful experience! Even if you're using your own homemade pipe jigs, it's mental anguish to leave one of your labor-of-love efforts as carpeting on the ocean floor.

With the heavy line you have a good chance of breaking the jig free. If it won't pull free with a strong pull from the direction you've hooked up, free-spool line and motor past the hang-up. Frequently the pull from the other direction will free the lure. Or, take a couple of turns on a rod holder or cleat and use the pull of the boat to break the jig free. If you're stuck that fast, free-spool enough line to allow your rod to lie on the bottom of the boat. Wrap a couple of turns on the rod holder or cleat and move off slowly, hoping that your jig will tear loose. Surprisingly, a jig can be freed in most cases using this method. You'll save a lure that you thought was a goner. More importantly, taking the stress of your line on the cleat or rod holder eliminates the distinct danger of breaking a rod. It might not stand the stress if you tried to hold onto the pole and pull the lure free by motoring away from the snag.

Fishing in these deeper waters requires more effort than shallow-water techniques, but if you're looking for lunker rockfish, this is where to start. Any rockfish taken from depth will have a ruptured air bladder from the rapid expansion of gases in his system as he is pumped to the surface. Therefore, fish caught in waters deeper than about 60 feet should always be killed and kept, as the fish will not survive if released. In some cases fish pumped up quickly from depths shallower than 60 feet may suffer decompression and have little chance of survival if released. This occurrence seems to be particularly true with China Rockfish which appear to be very fragile.

Don Dudley hoists the gaff on a Yellow Eye Rockfish for Fred Vander Werff.

CURRENTS AND TIDES

Tidal and current flow are significant factors in fishing the inside waters of Puget Sound, British Columbia, and southeast Alaska, where the tides can run at 7 or 8 knots in many areas. Even if you can get a jig or heavily weighted bait down, most rockfish are going to be lodged in the rocks or behind boulders. You'll get more hookups with the bottom than with fish when fishing under these conditions in medium depth and deeper.

These same locations, where you'll do nothing but donate terminal tackle to the underwater landscaping while tidal currents are running, can be hot and heavy action spots when the tide slacks its pace as it nears a high or low. This is the ideal time to fish the medium-level depths over 100 feet and as far down as 300 to 400 feet. You'll need special tackle to get down and into the strike zone with any efficiency (see Chapter Five following). On a good slack, it's possible to get down to 200 feet with 4 to 8 ounces quickly, which makes for much more enjoyable fishing than turning to cannonball leads of 16 to 48 ounces, which are frequently required for depths over 100 feet if the current is moving on the tide change. Good advice on fishing the midwater depths—if you can't hold your line on the bottom with 16 ounces, it's the signal to go to shallow-water techniques and move in where you can fish effectively. If the currents are too strong or the wind and current gang up on you to the point that you can't effectively fish shallow, it's time to hang things up and go home. Keep in mind that the fish will be there another day.

5

Deep-Water
(200 - 400 feet)
Fishing Techniques

DEEP-WATER bottom fishing pro-
vides the excitement and challenge of finding the big-
gest and most elusive heavyweights in northwest salt
water. The murky depths are the home range of Halibut, large Ling Cod, Yelloweye, Canary, and Boccacio
Rockfish.

Yelloweyes, Canary, Boccacio are the big three of
the rockfish family found in our waters. These red-
colored fish are often miscalled Red Snapper by most
fishermen, a misnomer since Red Snapper do not occur
north of Baja California. Other species encountered at
these depths are Quillback Rockfish, Pacific Cod, and
Walleye Pollack.

Deep-water fishing is a very specialized art, requiring special rods, reels, and lines and optimum
fishing conditions. This is where you'll catch your
trophy size rockfish, into the 20-pound class. Ling Cod
can run up to 70 pounds and Halibut up to 200. Halibut

actually get bigger, but landing a huge barn door is a nearly impossible task on rod and reel. For your trophy-sized fish, you'll have to pay a price. We call deep-water fishing the "grunt and groan sport!"

Pumping a large rockfish, Ling Cod, or Halibut from the depths is muscle-rending work. We've seen more than one angler break off a huge Halibut after 30 or 40 minutes of fighting it because they were too exhausted to battle the fish for the next hour or two needed to bring the fish to gaff.

If you really want to catch some big fish, by all means give deep-water fishing a try. We succumb to the temptation frequently, then retreat to shallow-water fishing to rest our aching muscles after boating a few big red rockfish and Ling Cod. Fishing at depths below 200 feet usually requires ideal weather and tidal conditions, as the task of getting to the bottom is all but impossible unless the wind is calm and tidal flow minimal. Ocean currents are often less than those encoutered on inside waters, but the weather factor on the open ocean can be the deep-water fisherman's first adversary in trying for trophy fish.

RODS, REELS, AND LINE

Special tackle designed to fish deep is almost a necessity. Heavy mooching tackle with monofilament line can be used, but the stretch in monofilament makes braided or wire line a better choice. A short, stiff, boat rod, large capacity reel, and 40- to 80-pound test braided *Dacron* or nylon line give you tackle capable of handling weights up to 32 ounces. Large jigs can also be worked effectively with this gear. Braided line does not have the durability of monofilament, so retie your knots frequently and check your line for worn spots. Using a McMahon snap swivel will save wear on the knot.

Wire line is about the only way to effectively fish all the way down to 400 feet and deeper. A braided wire outfit is neither inexpensive nor easy to use. We recommend this tackle for only the most determined bottom fishermen.

A boat rod with roller guides, a large capacity reel capable of holding 1000 feet of braided stainless steel wire (40- to 60-pound test) will cost about $80. The only reel we've seen that is readily available in most saltwater tackle shops that will handle wire line and the tremendous strain of weights up to 4 pounds is the *Penn 49M.*

Solid wire line is not a good choice for this kind of fishing as it kinks too easily. Roller guides are absolutely necessary with braided wire; any other line guides will be worn through in a day's fishing. The strain of 400 feet of wire line and up to a 4-pound cannon-ball sinker is too much to hold in two hands. The best quality rod holders are a must for this type of fishing. Minzer rod holders are somewhat expensive, but they are worth every penny. The simplest way to handle the whole outfit is to leave it in the rod holder while reeling up. This is not the most sporting type of fishing, but it the most effective manner for fishing at extreme depths. This method calls for a lot of hard work and is sometimes unproductive. But, the sight of a huge red shadow or a barn door halibut rising to the surface will erase all the fatigue.

TERMINAL TACKLE

Terminal tackle must be specially made for deepwater fishing. Wire line cannot be tied in knots but must be secured with metal sleeves for forming loops and securing swivels. Slide two metal sleeves up the end of the line, then form a loop, sliding the sleeves over the end of the loop and crimping the sleeves with pliers or special crimpers made for handling wire line. A good quality heavy-duty snap swivel should be rigged to the loop. You may wish to thread the line through the swivel eye when forming the loop prior to crimping.

You will need a wire spreader to keep your weight and heavy leader from tangling during its descent to the bottom. Without a spreader to separate the weight and leader, the leader will wrap around the main line and sinker as it is being freespooled. The result would be a tangled mass of line, leader and bait balled up on the end of your mainline. In this mess a fish would find it difficult to get at the bait if he had a pair of wire cutters. Without using a spreader, you'll spend more time undoing tangles than fishing. Spreaders of the size required are not commercially made at this writing; however, you'll find them easy to make following the steps in the accompanying illustration.

On the other arm attach a commercial quality rubber snubber. There is absolutely no stretch in wire line, making the snubber necessary to handle the stress of a heavy fish and to keep the fish from breaking off. On the end of the snubber tie a 60- to 80-pound test leader with 7/0 to 9/0 hooks. This may seem excessively heavy duty, but remember that this rig must be capable of handling Halibut over 100 pounds and Ling Cod over 50.

BAIT

Deep-water fish can be caught on large whole herring or live greenling bait as noted earlier. One tip to help your hook and bait stay off the bottom is to slide a large steelhead *Corkie* on the leader before securing the leader to the snubber. Place the *Corkie* just above the top hook, wrap a few turns of thread on the leader just above the *Corkie,* and tie it so the *Corkie* won't slide back up the leader. There are many variations and combinations that can be arranged on the leader.

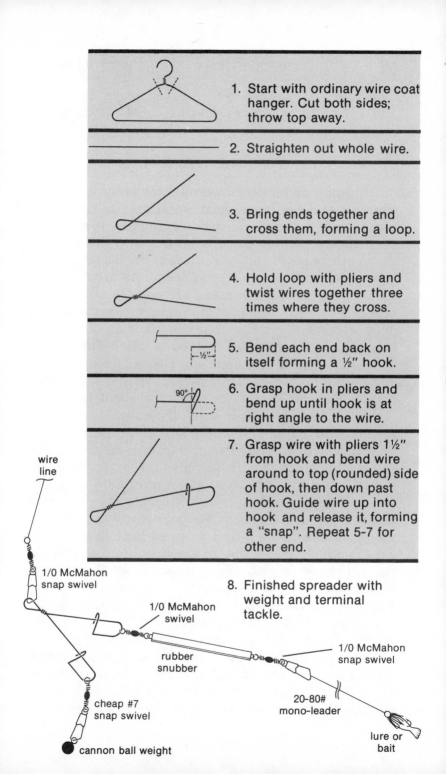

1. Start with ordinary wire coat hanger. Cut both sides; throw top away.

2. Straighten out whole wire.

3. Bring ends together and cross them, forming a loop.

4. Hold loop with pliers and twist wires together three times where they cross.

5. Bend each end back on itself forming a ½" hook.

6. Grasp hook in pliers and bend up until hook is at right angle to the wire.

7. Grasp wire with pliers 1½" from hook and bend wire around to top (rounded) side of hook, then down past hook. Guide wire up into hook and release it, forming a "snap". Repeat 5-7 for other end.

8. Finished spreader with weight and terminal tackle.

wire line

1/0 McMahon snap swivel

1/0 McMahon swivel

1/0 McMahon snap swivel

rubber snubber

20-80# mono-leader

cheap #7 snap swivel

cannon ball weight

lure or bait

One that has worked well for Yelloweye, Boccacio, and Ling Cod is a large peach colored *Corkie* and a white hoochie with a large whole herring on the hooks.

FISHING THE RIG

Rigging up for deep-water fishing is the easy part. Finding and fishing a deep water spot is the really tough task. A high quality depth sounder is almost a necessity in finding dropoffs, ridges, and shoals. Also the depth sounder can help prevent the loss of a lot of gear when drifting up a steep ledge. As in all bottom fishing, the productive areas are usually quite small and exact positioning is of major importance. Because deep water areas are sometimes far from shore, getting a good fix on your position is often difficult.

After finding the spot you suspect holds jumbo-sized bottom fish, you are ready. With your thumb tightly clamped on the side of the reel spool, throw the reel into free spool and carefully allow the 2- or 3-pound cannon-ball and bait to sink to the bottom. Use your thumb to prevent the spool from overrunning, because a backlash in wire line is a nightmare. Wire line is stiff and difficult to untangle. A minimum of experience will teach you how to avoid trouble. If you try this method, just remember as you pick away at your first major backlash, we didn't promise that this was an easy method. When the sinker hits bottom, quickly throw the reel in gear and wind up about three turns. Unless you possess the strength and stamina of King Kong, by all means put the rod in a holder. Keep one eye on your depth sounder screen and the other on the rod tip. If the depth changes, react accordingly. If the water suddenly becomes shallower, be ready to crank up to avoid getting snagged. If the bottom drops off, allow your sinker to drop down or you won't be close enough to the bottom to fish in the productive zone.

When your rod tip starts to signal a strike, set the hook by cranking up rapidly. Taking the rod out of the holder and trying to barb the fish by lifting the rod tip takes too much time. This maneuver also produces slack in the line and might allow the fish to shake off before you get him started toward the surface. We've had greater success hooking and landing these big fish by cranking the reel as fast as we can turn the handle.

The first time you experience a solid hookup with one of these big bottom dwellers, you'll be surprised at the strength of a big Yelloweye Rockfish or Ling Cod. If you choose to hold onto the rod, before you're through pulling up 200 to 400 feet of line and a struggling fish, you'll realize why we leave our rods in the holder during the entire battle. After landing your fish, dispatch him with a club, rebait, and get down to the bottom again, because the productive areas are usually small in size. When you hook your first fish, quickly observe your position and depth of water. These two factors are of primary importance when drifting over deep water. On more than one occasion we have forgotten to note these factors and after landing one fish were unable to relocate the hotspot.

If you're getting nibbles but no solid hookups, try feeding out a few feet of line after the first bite, then set the hook on the next tap. Sometimes the wind or tide will drift your bait too fast to allow the fish to get a good hold on it. Feeding out a little line to a subtle bite will often remedy this problem.

You'll need a lot of determination to go through all the effort involved in deep-water fishing. Most of this technique is nothing more than backbreaking work. Your effective fishing time is limited to the slack tide periods, and often the wind alone will negate any effort to fish deep.

We outline this method for those of you who are

really excited about catching trophy-sized bottom fish. Don't expect to go out and fill the fish box every time. The large Yelloweye Rockfish, Ling Cod, and Halibut are scarce even in the best areas. Always remember that bottom fish of this size are possibly 25 to 35 years old and cannot maintain their population under heavy fishing pressure.

If you decide to try deep-water fishing, don't leave your lighter tackle on shore; you'll need it on most days after the tide starts to run or the breeze comes up, ending your deep-water efforts for the day.

6

Caring For and Cooking Your Catch

IF THE fun is in the catching, the joy is in the eating.

Unfortunately, many times the catch is not properly cared for, and good fish ends up as inferior table fare. Many anglers simply throw their fish in the bottom of the boat, or only slightly better, an open fish box under the boat seat. By the time a day's fishing is done and you're back at the dock, the catch lies stiff and dry, still edible, but far from the quality a bit of care would have provided.

Your catch will provide far superior table fare if you follow these simple steps:

HANDLING AND CARING FOR THE CATCH

Immediately after landing a fish, rap it sharply on the head with a fish club, stunning the fish. Cut or break a gill arch to bleed the fish. Store the fish in a cooler with a layer of crushed ice on the bottom.

A good ice chest, at least a 30-quart size or larger, is a good investment that will last years and keep your fish in good condition. Once you've purchased an ice chest for a fish box, build a rack for the bottom of the cooler. Strips of wood or a section of plywood with supports underneath and holes bored throughout the surface allow water to drain from the melting ice. The rack should be about an inch above the bottom of the cooler to keep fish from lying in water at any time. Letting the fish lie in water allows them to soften, and the quality deteriorates quickly.

You need not layer each part of your catch with ice, as the ice on the bottom of the chest will adequately chill the catch for a day's fishing. However, you will want to ice your fish in layers if you're going to transport them some distance before cleaning.

The above steps accomplish three things: stunning stops the fish from flopping about in the box, activity which biologists have discovered builds up lac-

Quickly iced down after catching, a Blue Rockfish, Black Rockfish, and a small Ling Cod taken by jigging from the rocky shoreline on the Oregon Coast are prime food fish.

tic acid in the flesh as the fish is dying, causing deterioration of the eating quality of the fish. Bleeding drains nearly all the blood from the fish, which also produces a better, milder tasting piece of fish. Lastly, chilling keeps your catch cold and firm. Fish handled in this manner can be kept on ice for 2 or 3 days if necessary before filleting, steaking, or cleaning as whole fish.

Obviously, it's advantageous to clean your catch as soon as you're back at the dock. If you're skilled with a filleting knife and the water is not too rough, you can clean your catch on the ride back to the dock while your fishing partner handles the boat. On a long run, you can have your fillets packed in plastic bags and on ice by the time you're dockside. The carcasses may be discarded over the side. They become part of the ecological chain as food for other salt water creatures and organisms.

If you don't have the opportunity to clean your fish before getting home, here are a few suggestions for making it an easier, less messy job.

Get a good cutting board that will fit across a section of your kitchen or utility sink. A cutting board made from a good piece of birch will last for years. Plywood can be used if you take good care of it to prevent delamination. Sealing the side with varnish or fiberglass resin will stop delamination.

A 5- or 10-gallon bucket lined with a plastic trash can liner is ideal for depositing the carcasses as you clean or fillet. If you have space in your freezer, simply freeze all the carcasses in the bag until the day for garbage pickup when you can dispose of them with no fear of a mess or smell around the house. Better yet, package some of your carcasses in smaller bags and get yourself a crab pot that you can bait with your discards. Crabbing adds another seafood dimension to your diet!

Most of your catch will probably end up as fillets, although whole fish, roasts, and steaks are all something to consider when cleaning your catch.

Many fishermen have a basic idea on filleting fish. There is more than one effective method. For boneless fillets, here's one way of preparing rockfish, Cod, and Lings.

FILLETING

To begin with, you should have the proper tools—a good flexible filleting knife with an 8- to 10-inch blade, whetstone of medium grit, fine whetstone, such as an Arkansas hardstone, and ideally, if you're handling lots of fish, a good steel to keep the edge on your knife as you work. A heavier thick-bladed butcher knife is well worth the investment for handling larger fish where you're severing bones when deheading or steaking. Generally the filleting knives sold at most sporting good stores are not as sturdy as a good commercial grade filleting or butcher knife sold at outlets for commercial fishermen. Ask your dealer if he

A good quality filleting knife and cutting board are necessary tools for processing your catch.

carries or can order a commercial grade knife, such as a Ullis or Dexter-Russell. Since a good filleting knife should last for years, a dollar or two more for a better quality knife is money well spent. Don't even consider a cheap filleting knife if you're going to become a serious bottom fisherman.

You'll save yourself many painful nicks and cuts inflicted by the spines that are part of a rockfish's anatomy if you use a pair of gloves when handling your fish. Use the gloves from the time you unhook the fish and place it in the ice chest through filleting or other cleaning. Rubberized cloth gloves are well worth the couple of dollars they cost.

1. To begin filleting, lay the fish on its side, backside toward you. Cut right behind the head in a diagonal cut down to the backbone.

2. Turn your knife and slide the blade along the backbone toward the tail.

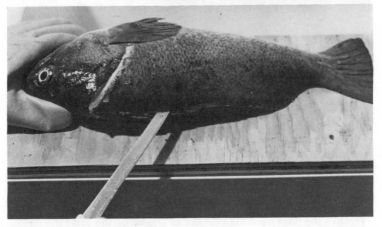

3. Your blade tip should cut right along the rib cage, then thrust all the way through the fish at the vent and continue to slide your blade towards the tail, keeping the knife blade flat against the backbone.

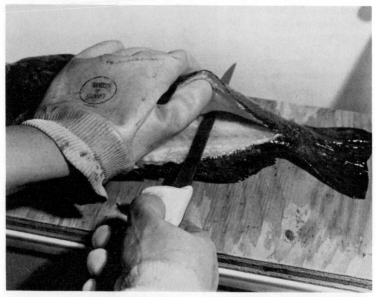

4. As you reach the tail, you have 2 choices—either invert the knife and begin your return cut, leaving the skin attached at the tail as in photo above, or cutting through the skin at the tail to remove the fillet from the carcass as shown on the opposite page.

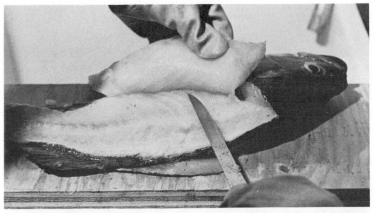

5.   Invert your knife running it back towards the head, depressing the knife handle so that the blade will flex and the tip will ride over the rib cage in a clean motion.

6.   Cut through the skin along the belly section and rib cage, freeing the fillet from the carcass.

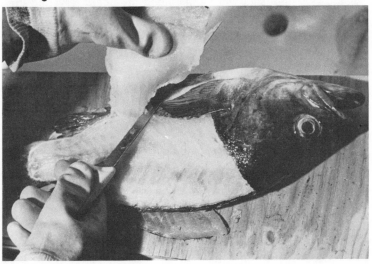

7.   If you've cut the fillet free at the tail with your stroke from head to tail, you can either skin the fish at this time or lay it aside for skinning when you've taken all the fillets.

8.   If you've left the fillet attached at the fish's tail, flop the fillet so that it lays over the tail on your cutting board. Holding the carcass, fillet close to the edge of the board, cut down to the edge of the skin, and slide your knife along the board, severing the fillet from the skin in a single, smooth stroke.

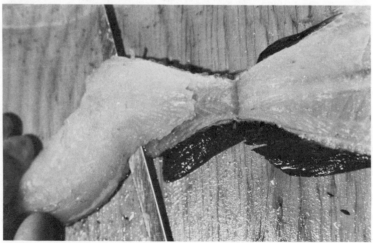

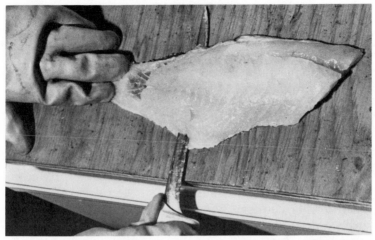

9.   If you've removed and stacked your fillets, begin your skinning cut at the tail end of the fillet, holding the end of the fillet with 2 fingers about 1/2 inch from the end of the fillet and use the same single-stroke cutting method as described for skinning with the skin left attached to the tail.

10.   Finished fillets. Cabezon and Ling Cod frequently have blue flesh. Don't be alarmed by this coloration; it's a natural condition and the flesh turns white when cooked.

COOKING

Many Northwest anglers will tell you that when it comes to eating, they prefer bottom fish to salmon.

Our experience is that each individual fish has its own flavor characteristics, and cooking methods can enhance or in some cases lessen the quality of the table fare. Some bottom fish are excellent regardless of how you can cook them; others are definitely more tasteful steamed or broiled than deep-fat fried.

Cookbooks are filled with fish recipes, many complicated and time consuming, so we're dealing only with simple cookery you can do at home or with the rudimentary equipment found in many fishing resorts near salt water areas.

Basically there are four methods of preparing your catch: baking, broiling, steaming, and frying. Most people are used to frying their fillets. Although fresh fish and chips will never be turned down at our homes, we feel that there are other methods that in many ways are preferable to frying.

Frying

If you wish to fry your fillets, follow these simple directions for home or camp cookery. Rinse fresh fillets lightly, pat dry with paper towels, and coat with a good batter mix.

Batter Mix

If you have the time to make your own batter mix, here's one that we like:

2 cups flour
1 teaspoon salt
1 teaspoon baking powder
1 egg
1 or 2 cups milk or a 12-ounce can of beer (we prefer the beer)
1 tablespoon shortening or cooking oil

Sift flour, salt, and baking powder together. Then add egg, liquid, and shortening or oil. Mix the batter thoroughly until smoothly blended. Dip fillets in batter and deep fry in cooking oil or shortening at about 375 degrees until browned. The fillets should be cooked through, with a light batter coating sealing in the juices of the fish. You should have a crisp batter coating with moist, flaky fillets inside.

For those who don't want to mess around with measuring and preparing a batter, here's a quick and simple alternative. Add liquid per directions to a package of Tempura Batter mix for frying fish. It will save time and give you the same results as a hand-mixed batter. A mix is especially handy when cooking on a fishing trip where you'll probably not want to carry all the separate ingredients plus a sifter.

Steaming

Steaming fish is one of the simplest and tastiest methods you can use either for fillets, whole sole, or whole rockfish.

Simple steaming or poaching is done with a frying pan by adding a bit of water to simmer the fish in. Bring water to a boil; cover the fillets with a pan lid, and allow the fish to simmer in its own juices for 6 to 7 minutes. Cooking time is best judged by checking to see if the flesh is beginning to separate, indicating that it's cooked through. Fish should be cooked just enough to flake easily with the touch of a fork. Overcooking loses some of the delicate flavor of a properly cooked piece of fish.

Salt and pepper lightly during the steaming process for seasoning. If you want to get a little fancy, substitute white wine for water to begin steaming the fish. Sliced onions, green peppers, and mushrooms give your dish added taste.

Chinese Steamed Rockfish

Traditional Chinese steamed rockfish with various sauces is a super treat. This method requires the preparation of sauces, and since the fish is cooked with all scales carefully removed but head and fins still attached, some diners may not find the sight on the platter as pleasing as skinned and headed whole fish or fillets. If those dining at your table will not be bothered by the cooked fish's appearance, by all means try the following recipe, which is from a National Marine Fisheries Service bulletin.

2-3 lb. rockfish
1-2 green onions sliced finely lengthwise
3 tablespoons ginger root sliced finely in 3″-4″
lengths
1 cup soy sauce
3 cups water
1 drop sesame oil (not too much; it is strong)
onion, chopped
parsley

Place green onions, ginger root, soy sauce, water, and sesame oil in saucepan, and simmer for 30 minutes. Leave head and fins on gutted and scaled rockfish. Bring water to a hard boil in a covered steamer (enough water to cover bottom and not touch fish). Put chopped onion and parsley in cavity, and place rockfish on rack in steamer. Steam for 7 to 10 minutes. Fish should be moist and flaky. Place fish on a platter, make several cuts in its skin, pour on sauce, and serve. Serves 2 to 4.

Steamed Fish Fillet Sandwiches

Cut fillets of rockfish, Ling Cod, or cod in sections that will fit onto a slice of bread. Place your fillets in a lightly buttered frying pan and simmer to brown the sides, then add enough water to steam cook the fish at a medium temperature.

While the fillets are steaming in a covered frying pan, butter up enough slices of bread for the number of fillets you're cooking. Add a slice of cheddar cheese and tartar sauce spread on your second slice of bread, and wait until the fillets are cooked. Lightly season the fillets and as soon as they are steamed through, put your sandwiches together and dig in!

Boiled Sole

We were introduced to boiled sole and potatoes many years ago on a research vessel working in northern California sampling trawl fisheries resources. The boat's cook was a seasoned hand with many years aboard commercial fishing boats plying the West Coast waters. Though his name has long been forgotten, his cooking surely hasn't. Our thanks to this galley master who set the boat's mess with this simple but memorable and oft repeated meal:

Boil enough potatoes to yield a full serving per person; if you can get them, new potatoes are best. The number of potatoes used will depend on the appetites of the diners, so use your own judgment here.

After you've put the potatoes on to boil, place a whole sole, headed and cleaned, in a frying pan with enough water to completely cover the bottom of the pan, but not so much that the fish is covered completely by water. Salt and pepper lightly. Bring the water to a boil, cover the pan, then reduce the heat and simmer until the fish is done. Test by inserting a fork in the cooking fish. Plan your timing so that the potatoes will be fully cooked when you're ready to serve the fish. Depending on the appetites of those at the table, plan on 1 to 2 sole per person.

Serve up your sole, boiled potatoes, with melted butter, green peas or another green vegetable, and salad, and you'll have a happy crew whether they're aboard ship or have both feet planted firmly on solid ground.

Boiling sole is basically a method of steam cooking, since you are using just enough water to keep the fish from burning in the pan as it is cooked by the simmering water.

Broiling

Baking or broiling requires an oven or, if you're on an outing, cooking on or in foil over a charcoal fueled barbecue or hibachi.

One of our favorite methods of preparing Ling Cod, a fish which can be cooked in almost any manner and be a palate pleaser, is to broil it.

Cut a roast from a Ling Cod fillet with the skin left on if it's a larger fish—anything over 10 pounds. Otherwise, take a full fillet and place it in foil with the skin side down. Coat the flesh liberally with butter, sprinkle salt and pepper, and pop in under the broiler unit about 4 to 6 inches below the broiling element.

Cook until the butter has boiled and has formed a brown crusty coating over the top of the fish. At this point the fish will be cooked completely through. On larger chunks of fish, it's best to have the broiling tray 6 inches from the heating element to allow slower cooking, so that the fish will be cooked all the way through without burning the crust. The fish will be moist and flaky inside with the layer of browned butter sealing in these juices. Again, it's ideally done when the fish flakes off with the touch of a fork. Delicious!

If you're cooking on a barbecue, you won't be able to attain this crust and your fish will be more like lightly baked fish.

Baking

For baking, wrap a roast section or several fillets in foil with butter, salt, and pepper. Cook at about 400 degrees for about 15 minutes on one side, using a broiler pan under the foil to hold the juices that you'll drain from the foil-encased fish. After about 15 minutes, take a fork and puncture the foil about every 2 inches and turn the package over, allowing excess fluid to drain from the package and cook for another 5 minutes.

Use the same procedure for cooking over charcoal. Cooking time for a roast or fillets of 2 pounds take about the same time as cooking in an oven. However, you may want to experiment on your cooking times to suit your preference.

Soup

Now that the basic cooking techniques are covered, here's an additional treat that will yield extra meals, quickly and simply cooked, and give you a chance to use those extra scrap bits of fish that you miss in filleting.

With your filleting knife, take time to trim any pieces of flesh that are left on the carcass. Usually they are bits where you let your knife ride too high along the bone as you made your cut towards the tail. On larger bottom fish such as Lings, large rockfish, and Cabezon, carefully carve out the flesh from the back of the head. Remove the cheeks, which are located in a pocket just below the eye and forward of the gills on the upper jaw. These tidbits are delicious and shouldn't be wasted. Pack one or two cups of these small scrap-sized cuts in small plastic sandwich bags and store them on the freezer shelf of your refrigerator.

Throw It Together Fish Soup

A small bag of fish scraps, a can of soup, and a few vegetables will make a gourmet soup that is better than the soups and chowders you'll get at most seafood restaurants.

1-2 cups frozen fish scraps or small fillets
sliced potatoes
green onions or leeks
celery or green pepper
1 can tomato or potato soup
1-2 cups milk
butter, salt, and pepper

Take a frozen package of fish scraps or small fillets and place it in a large soup pan with a cup or slightly more of water and bring to a boil. Add sliced potatoes, green onions or leeks, and celery or green peppers if you wish. Simmer for about 45 minutes.

When the frozen fish is thawed as it cooks, add one can of tomato soup but no additional water. You may wish to substitute potato soup as an alternative. Add 1 or 2 cups milk, a couple of tablespoons of butter, and salt and pepper to taste. Heat until the milk is hot but not boiling. Serve it now and be prepared to serve seconds. Serves 2 to 4 persons depending on how hungry they are.

If your fish is not frozen, cook your vegetables first, adding the fish a few minutes before the canned soup and milk. You want your fish just cooked through.

With rolls or garlic bread and a green salad, it's a full dinner in itself!

7

Making Your Own Lures

As A dedicated bottom fisherman, you may find it worth your while to mold your own jigs. You might also consider molding your own plastic worms. Making your own lures offers both the satisfaction of catching fish with lures you've personally made and economic benefits in that once you have

Two example of jigs. (Bottom) Jig will work fine with just a plastic worm threaded on the hook. For more action, (top) bucktail deer hair, bear hair, or artificial hair can be tied on the collar with size A nylon thread.

the basic equipment, individual jig costs are far below those of commercially manufactured and prepackaged jigs you'll buy from fishing tackle outlets.

Since most of the small leadhead jigs available in retail outlets are freshwater bass lures, they are made with hooks that will not stand up to the abuses of salt-water. Cadmium plated or tinned hooks are the only reasonable answer to saltwater. Stainless steel jig hooks are the best available, however are not readily available and are quite costly in comparison to cadmium or tinned hooks.

While molding leadheads you may wish to make a few deepwater jigs. The easiest is the pipe jig which can be made from copper, stainless steel, or aluminum tubing. Molds and hooks are available from mail order catalogs in any variety of styles and weights. Lead can be purchased at hardware stores or from automotive garages that remove old wheel balancing weights. Follow these simple steps to safe and trouble-free jig making.

1) Melt lead in production hot pot or in a ladle over gas burner or propane torch. Be sure there is good ventilation as the fumes can be dangerous. Also arrange a time when you can work in an area clear of all children and pets.

2) After the lead is molten, wearing gloves, use an old spoon to skim off all the slag from the top.

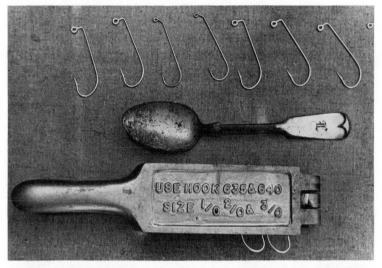

3) Spread out all the hooks in a clear area where they are easily handled. Preheat the mold by pouring once with no hooks in the cavities.

4) Position hooks in the slots and close the mold.

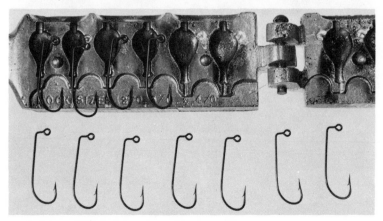

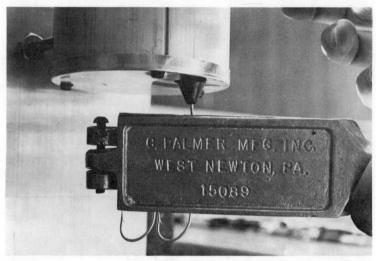

5) Pour the lead carefully but rapidly so it will completely fill each cavity.

6) Remove the finished jig with gloves or pliers to avoid burns and place them aside to cool on a plank of wood. Refill the mold with hooks and repeat the procedure.

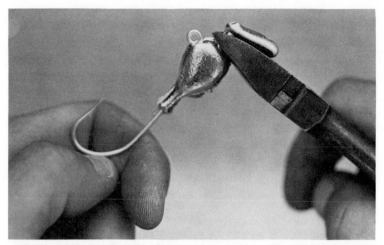

7) After the jig heads have cooled, remove the excess lead left at the pouring spout with side cutters. Scraps can be remelted to make more jigs.

8) Trim edges of jig heads with a sharp knife and (9) smooth with a file.

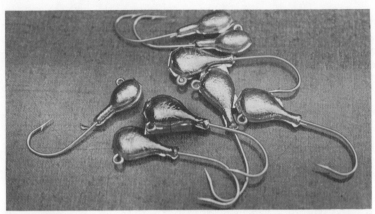

10) Jigs can be used as cast or painted with good quality lead epoxy paint. Enamel paint should be avoided, as it will chip off or soften from chemical action of contact with rubber skirts or plastic worms.

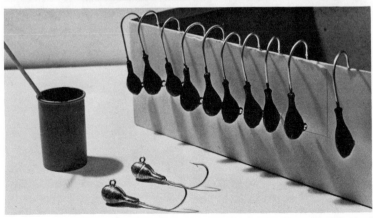

13) For a bucktail tie on a bunch of hair, allowing it to slip around the collar until it is evenly distributed on all sides. Then tie it down and trim the excess.

14) Fiber weedguards of polypropylene rope can be tied in on top of the finished wrapping for weedless jigs.

15) A good alternative to tying hair is to slip durable rubber or vinyl skirts on the collar to add action and color to the jig.

PIPE JIGS

Pipe jigs are easy to make, are effective deep-water jigs, and require very little investment. Copper pipe of 1/2- to 3/4-inch diameter is about the right size. Begin by heating lead and skimming the slag as shown earlier (page 112).

16) Fill a can (1- or 2-pound coffee cans are ideal) half full of sand. Place one end of the pipe in the sand and pour molten lead into the pipe. After all pipes are full, set aside to cool. Copper pipe filled with hot lead retains heat for a lengthy period of time, so be careful.

17) After the pipe has cooled, cut it into desired lengths with a hacksaw. Your jig will have more action if you cut the pipe on a 45-degree diagonal.

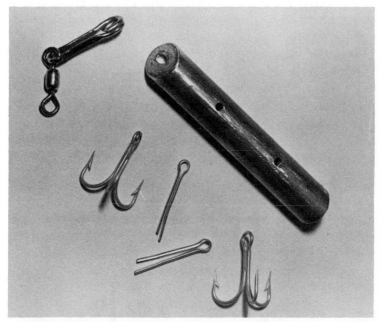

18) **Here is one of the best ways to attach the hooks and swivels to the jig. Drill 3 holes in the pipe as follows: First hole is to attach a split ring or large snap swivel; drill about 1/4 inch down from one end. The 2nd and 3rd holes are to attach hooks. Drill a hole near the bottom but through both sides of the pipe. Check the length of the treble hook and locate the hole high enough for the end of the jig to touch bottom before the hook. Drill the second hole about the same distance from the top.**

19) **Put your treble hooks into large cotter keys and slip them through the holes so the hooks hang on opposite sides of the pipe.**

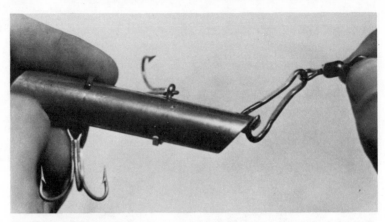

20) With a large split ring or commercial grade snap swivel through the top hole, your homemade jig is ready to fish.

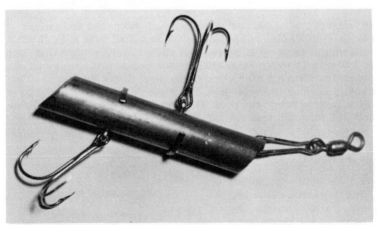

21) Some fishermen prefer the dark oxidized finish on the copper pipe, but if that doesn't work, a scouring pad will shine the pipe to a bright finish.

PLASTIC WORMS

Plastic worms are easy and inexpensive to make, however since they are fairly inexpensive items when bought in bulk, you may find your efforts better directed in making jigs and buying your worms. One distinct advantage of molding your own worms is that you can be assured that you're going to have worms with the toughness required to stand up to the battering that bottom fish in a hungry mood will do to your lure. Plastic worms made for bass fishing tend to be softer in texture and may not hold up well. When you make your own, you can add a hardener to make a more durable lure.

We've outlined the procedures for "making your own" as follows.

22) Materials for molding plastic worms: Plastic, molds, colors, pouring pot, and heater (kitchen stove may be used).

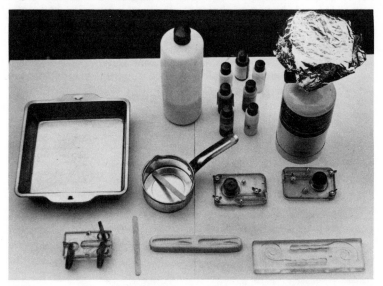

23) Shake the plastic liquid until no residue is visible on the bottom of the bottle. Pour into a small pot with a pouring spout. Do not fill over 1/2 full; small quantities are easier to work with. Any scrap or old worms may also be remelted. If a gas burner is used, make a pad of several layers of aluminum foil and place it between the flame and pouring pan. Direct gas flame will scorch the plastic on the bottom of the pan.

24) Heat the plastic liquid to about 325 degrees Fahrenheit. It will turn clear and thicken to the consistency of syrup. Stir frequently and avoid over heating. Plastic liquid is easily scorched. Work in a well ventilated area. Add color to the melted plastic while stirring. Start with small amounts of color and add drops until desired shade is reached. If a softer worm is desired, plastic softener may be added after heating. Fluorescent colors will be brighter if added before plastic is heated. Plastic hardener should also be added before heating.

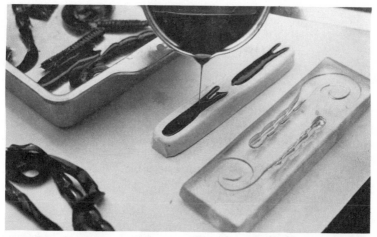

25) Pour the plastic into molds. Flat molds are easier to work with, but injector molds produce a full, round worm. Wipe the spout of pouring pan to prevent plastic drips from scorching on the burner.

26) Allow the worm to cool for about 1 minute, then carefully remove worm from mold. The finished worm can be placed in a shallow pan of water for final cooling. Do not allow any water in the mold as hot plastic will splatter on contact with water.

SOURCES OF MATERIALS

Ament Mold Co.
402 Capelle
Grain Valley, MO 64029

Hopkins Fishing Lures Co.
1130 Boissevain Ave.
Norfolk, VA 23507

M-F Manufacturing Co.
P.O. Box 13442
Fort Worth, TX 76118

Midland Tackle Co.
66 Rt. 17
Sloatsburg, NY 10974

Okiebug Distributing Co.
3501 S. Sheridan
Tulsa, OK 74145

Reed Tackle
Box 1348
Fairfield, NJ 07006

The Tackle Shop
Limit Manufacturing Corp.
Box 369
Richardson, TX 75080

8

Common Species Available

THIS SECTION lists some of the most common species of bottom fish encountered by the sports fisherman. Many other species inhabit Northwest waters but are rarely seen by fishermen. This general guide answers the usual question, "What is it?"

ROCKFISH FAMILY: *Scorpaenidae*

Copper Rockfish *Sebastes caurinus*
Alias: rockcod

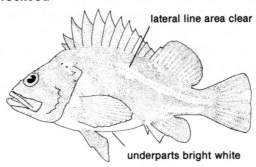

lateral line area clear

underparts bright white

The Copper Rockfish has dark brown back with yellow splashed sides, often seen with two yellow bands radiating from the eye over the cheek patch. The posterior half of the lateral line is usually light colored. The belly is white. Coppers are distributed from southern California to the Bering Sea at depths of very shallow to 200 feet. Their food items include: crabs, clams, sculpins, blennies, shiner perch and shrimp. Herring are only rarely eaten.

Brown Rockfish *Sebastes auriculatus*
Alias: rockcod

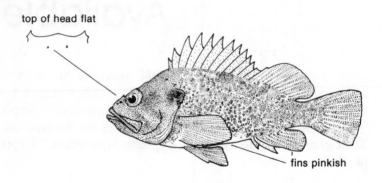

top of head flat

fins pinkish

The Brown Rockfish is light brown, mottled with dark brown, and dusky pink fins. The lateral line is usually pinkish. Browns are distributed from Baja California to southeast Alaska but are relatively rare north of Puget Sound and on coastal Washington. Browns seem to be limited by colder water temperatures of the San Juan Islands and the Strait of Juan de Fuca. Found in depths of 40 to 150 feet deep. Food items include: shrimp, sculpins, and small crustaceans.

Quillback Rockfish *Sebastes malinger*

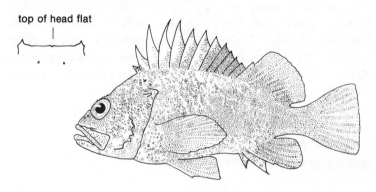

top of head flat

The Quillback Rockfish is brown to dark brown with yellow mottling on dorsal fin, back, and sides. The Quillback usually has characteristic black freckles on its cheeks. The Quillback is distributed from central California to the Gulf of Alaska, in water very shallow to 600 feet deep. In the northern part of its range they tend to be abundant in shallow (20 to 50 feet) water. Food items include: shrimp, crabs, clams, worms, perch, sculpins, and various small crustaceans.

Black Rockfish *Sebastes melanops*
Alias: Black Sea Bass, Black Bass

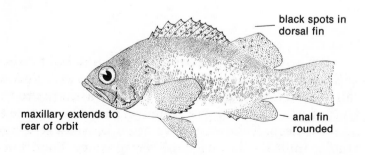

black spots in
dorsal fin

maxillary extends to
rear of orbit

anal fin
rounded

The Black Rockfish is black on the back becoming mottled gray on the sides with a white belly. Blacks are distributed from southern California to the Gulf of Alaska. They inhabit areas from the surface to 300 feet of water, often found in midwater. Food items include: small herring, candlefish, perch, shrimp, and various small crustaceans.

Yellowtail Rockfish *Sebastes flavidus*
Alias: green snapper, brown bomber

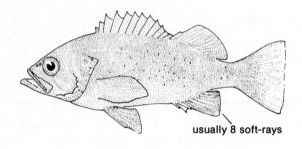

usually 8 soft-rays

Yellowtail Rockfish are olive green to light brown with characteristic faded yellow fins and tail. Yellowtails are distributed from San Diego, California to the Gulf of Alaska. They can be found from the surface to 300 feet deep. Yellowtails are often in midwater, and studies indicate they are highly migratory. Food items include: herring, candlefish, lantern fish, shrimp, squid, and various crustaceans.

Boccacio *Sebastes paucispinis*
Alias: Rock Salmon

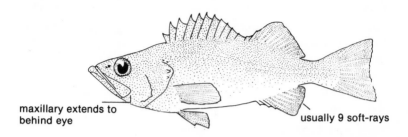

maxillary extends to
behind eye

usually 9 soft-rays

The Boccacio is dusky red on the back, silvery red on sides, and pink belly. They are easily identified by their oversized mouth. Boccacio are distributed from Baja California to the Gulf of Alaska; relatively rare north of Washington. They are found at depths of 150 to 600 feet. Food items include various fish.

Canary Rockfish *Sebastes pinniger*

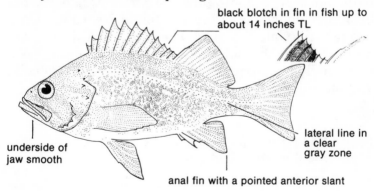

black blotch in fin in fish up to
about 14 inches TL

underside of
jaw smooth

lateral line in
a clear
gray zone

anal fin with a pointed anterior slant

The Canary Rockfish is vividly colored, pale orange on back, mottled with gray on the sides, lighter on belly. All the fins and tail are bright orange. Canaries are distributed from Baja California to southeast Alaska at depths from 200 to 800 feet deep. Food items include various fish.

Yelloweye Rockfish *Sebastes ruberrimus*
Alias: Rasphead, Red Snapper, Turkey Red Rockfish, Cowcod

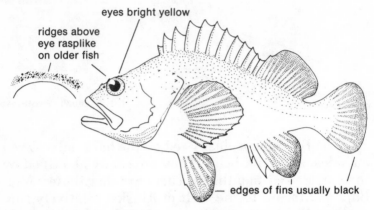

eyes bright yellow

ridges above eye rasplike on older fish

edges of fins usually black

Yelloweye Rockfish are bright orange to yellow orange on the back with pinkish tones on the sides and pale belly. The fins are pink, sometimes edged with black. The distinguishing characteristic is the brilliant yellow eye. They are found from Baja California to the Gulf of Alaska. They are found at depths of 80 to 800 feet. Found shallower in open ocean. Food items include: herring, Pacific Cod, Dogfish, Pollack, and other fish.

COD FAMILY: *Gadidae*

Pacific Cod *Gadus macrocephalus*
Alias: True Cod, Gray Cod

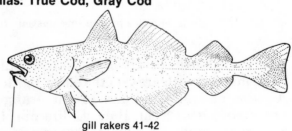

gill rakers 41-42

barbel longer than diameter of eye
(rarely slightly shorter)

Pacific Cod are brown to gray on the back with numerous brown spots on back and sides with light belly. Pacific Cod have a characteristic whisker on the tip of the lower jaw and three separate dorsal fins. Pacific Cod are distributed from Santa Monica, California to the Bering Sea and Japan. They are found in water 20 to 600 feet deep. Cod school in shallower water to spawn in the winter months. Food items include: worms, crabs, molluscs, shrimp, herring, candlefish, Walleye Pollack, and flatfish.

Walleye Pollack *Theragra chalcogrammus*

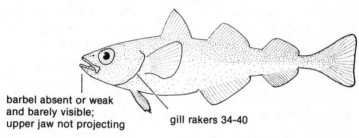

barbel absent or weak
and barely visible;
upper jaw not projecting   gill rakers 34-40

Walleye Pollack are olive green to brown mottled on the back, with silvery sides and light belly. They have a big eye and protruding lower jaw; no whisker. Pollack are distributed from central California to the Bering Sea and Sea of Japan. They are found at depths of 50 to 600 feet and are common in shallower water in the winter months. Food items include: herring, candlefish, and shrimp.

Tom Cod *Microgadus proximus*

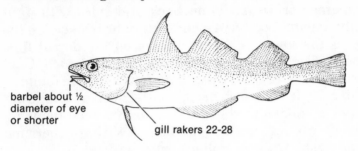

barbel about ½
diameter of eye
or shorter

gill rakers 22-28

The Tom Cod is uniformly brown to olive green on the back with creamy sides and belly. Tod Cod have a whisker at the tip of the lower jaw and three separate dorsal fins. They can be distinguished from Pacific Cod by their lack of spotting and small size. Tom Cod rarely exceed 12 inches in length. They are distributed from central California to the Gulf of Alaska and the Bering Sea. They inhabit depths of 20 to 600 feet. Their food items include: various shrimp and small crustaceans.

Pacific Hake *Merluccius productus*

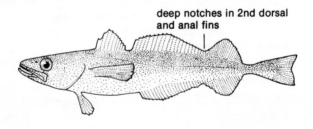

deep notches in 2nd dorsal
and anal fins

Hake are dark or metallic silver gray with black speckling on the belly and sides. They are distinguished from the other cod by the black lining in the mouth, large teeth, and a lack of whisker on the lower jaw. Hake are distributed from the Gulf of California to the Gulf of Alaska. They are found from the surface to 1000 feet deep. Evidence seems to suggest they are most active at night and closest to the surface, returning to the depths in the daytime. Their food items include: shrimp, candlefish, and herring.

SABLEFISH FAMILY: *Anoplopomatidae*

Sablefish *Anoplopoma fimbria*
Alias: Black Cod

17-30 spines in 1st dorsal

widely spaced dorsal fins

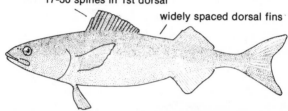

Sablefish are slate black to greenish gray on the back, shading to light gray on the belly. Younger fish up to 2 feet long are often much lighter in color. Sablefish are distributed from Baja California to the Bering Sea and Japan. Adults are found in water deeper than 600 feet. Juveniles are found in shallower waters of Puget Sound, the Strait of Juan de Fuca, and Straits of Georgia. Their food items include: lantern fish, crustaceans, worms, and other small fish.

GREENLING FAMILY: *Hexagramidae*

Ling Cod *Ophiodon elongatus*

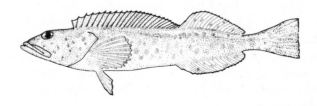

The Ling Cod has dark mottling on the back and sides that can be brown, gray or green depending on environment. They are usually paler on the belly. Ling Cod are recognized by their elongated body, large head, and mouth full of sharp teeth. Ling Cod are distributed from Baja California to Kodiak, Alaska. They can be found from the surface to 600 feet deep. Ling Cod are voracious feeders, and their food items include: flounders, hake, Walleye Pollack, cod, and rockfishes. They are also cannibalistic.

Whitespotted Greenling *Hexagrammos stelleri*

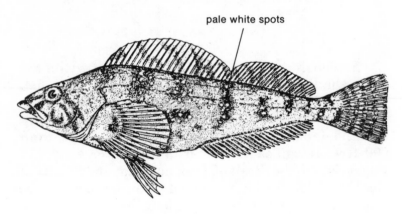

pale white spots

Whitespotted Greenling are light brown to greenish with dusky blotches or bars on the sides. There are conspicuous small white spots on the body. They are distributed from Oregon to the Bering Sea and Japan. They are found in shallow areas along rocky shores. Their food items include: worms, crustaceans, and small fishes.

Kelp Greenling *Hexagrammos decragrammus*

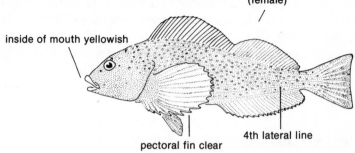

(female)

inside of mouth yellowish

pectoral fin clear

4th lateral line

   The Kelp Greenling exhibits distinct coloration
between sexes. The female is gray-brown with bright
golden to light brown spots on body and head. The
male is dark gray with bright blue spots on head and
sides. Kelp Greenling are distributed from La Jolla,
California to the Aleutian Islands, Alaska. They are
not commonly found in Puget Sound. They are found
from intertidal to 150 feet, common in kelp beds, and
along rocky shorelines. Their food items include:
worms, crustaceans, and small fishes.

SCULPIN FAMILY: *Cottidae*

Cabezon *Scorpaenichthys marmoratus*

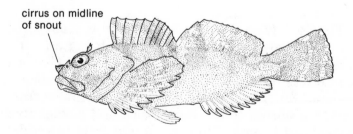

cirrus on midline
of snout

The Cabezon is olive green to brown or gray mottled with lighter areas. Coloration is variable with environment. Cabezon are recognized by their large head, thick lips, and wide pectoral fins. They are distributed from Baja California to southeast Alaska. They are found often from very shallow water to depths of 150 feet. Their diet is almost exclusively crabs.

Red Irish Lord *Hemilepidotus hemilepidotus*

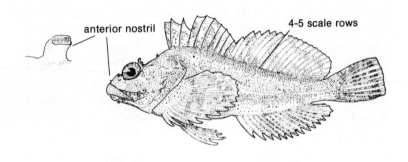

anterior nostril

4-5 scale rows

The Red Irish Lord has a bright to dusky red back with brown, white and black mottling all over. There are usually 4 dark bars on the sides. The Red Irish Lord is recognized by 4 rows of scales just below the dorsal fin. The Red Irish Lord is distributed from central California to the Bering Sea and Kamchatka Peninsula of Russia. They are found from intertidal to 150 feet deep. Their food items include: crabs, barnacles, and mussels.

FLATFISH FAMILY: *Bothidae*—Lefteye Flounders

Pacific Sanddab *Citharichthys sordidus*

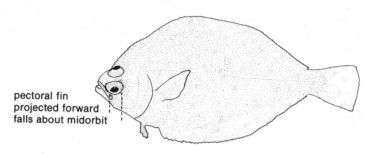

pectoral fin
projected forward
falls about midorbit

The Sanddab is a left-eyed flounder, colored dull brown to tan with darker mottling on the eyed side, off white to pale brown on the blind side. The Pacific Sanddab is recognized as the only common left-eyed flounder encountered in Northwest waters. They also have a bony knob under the jaw. Their distribution extends from Baja California to the Bering Sea. They are found in depths of 30 to 900 feet. Pacific Sanddab feed on herring, candlefish, worms, and other invertebrates.

FAMILY *Pleuronectidae*—Righteye Flounders

Pacific Halibut *Hippoglossus stenolepis*

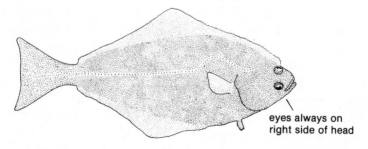

eyes always on
right side of head

Halibut are dark brown to gray with lighter mottling on the eyed side and white on the blind side. The Halibut is recognized by its white underside, a firm, muscular body, and large size. Halibut are distributed from southern California into the Bering Sea. They inhabit depths from 20 to 1200 feet. Their food items include various fishes, crabs, clams, squid, and other invertebrates.

Rock Sole *Lepidopsetta bilineata*

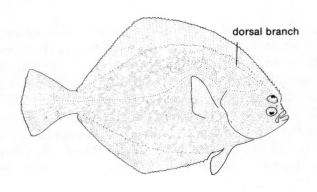

dorsal branch

The Rock Sole is dark brown with lighter or darker mottling on the eyed side, off white on the blind side. Color is extremely variable with location. Rock Sole are recognized by their small mouth and dorsal branch off the lateral line. Their range extends from southern California to the Bering Sea and Japan. They are found at depths of 20 to 600 feet. Common in shallow water in the summer months. Their food items include: mollusc siphons, clams, polychaete worms, shrimp, small crabs, brittle stars, and candlefish.

Starry Flounder *Platichthys stellatus*

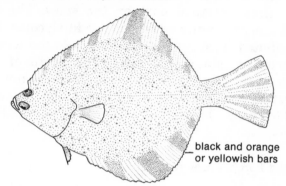

black and orange
or yellowish bars

The Starry Flounder is dark brown to black on the eyed side, white with black blotching on the blind side. They are found either right- or left-eyed. They are easily recognized by their rough patches of scales and alternating light and dark bands on their fins. Starry Flounder are distributed from southern California to the Bering Sea and Japan. They are found in water very shallow to 450 feet deep—often in brackish water in river mouths and estuaries. Their food items include: crabs, shrimp, clams, and small molluscs.

PERCH FAMILY: *Embiotocidae*

Redtail Surfperch *Amphistichus rhodoterus*

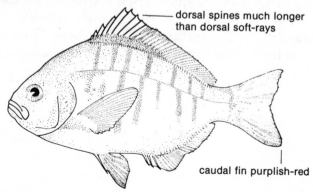

dorsal spines much longer
than dorsal soft-rays

caudal fin purplish-red

The Redtail Surfperch has a silvery body with olive green vertical bars on the sides. The tail and anal fins are characteristically reddish color. They are distributed from central California to the west side of Vancouver Island and inside the Strait of Juan de Fuca on the Olympic Peninsula. They are not found in Puget Sound. Redtails are found from the surface to 24 feet deep. Their food items include small crustaceans.

Striped Perch *Embiotoca lateralis*

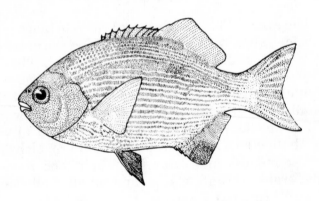

The Striped Perch is coppery brown with horizontal blue stripes on the sides. Their distribution extends from Baja California to Port Wrangell, Alaska. They are found from the surface to 55 feet deep. Their food items include: small crustaceans, worms, mussels, and herring eggs.

Pile Perch *Rhacochilus vacca*

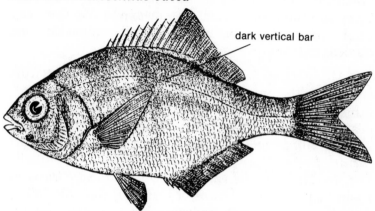

dark vertical bar

    Pile Perch are silvery with blackish back and a dark vertical bar on the sides. They have a deeply forked tail and dusky fins. Pile Perch are distributed from northern Baja California to southeast Alaska. They are commonly associated with piers and pilings. They are also found in water up to 150 feet deep. They feed on mussels, barnacles, and small crustaceans.

Shiner Perch *Cymatogaster aggregata*

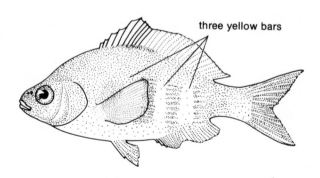

three yellow bars

    Shiner Perch are silver in color with three vertical yellow bars. They are noted for their small size, maximum of 6 inches long. Shiner Perch are found from northern Baja California to Port Wrangell, Alaska. They inhabit water from the surface to 250 feet deep. Their food items include: copepods, mussels, barnacles, and algae.

This section outlines general guidelines to identify some of the most common species—undoubtedly others will be encountered. If the reader is seriously searching for positive identification, we suggest consulting *Guide to the Coastal Marine Fishes of California,* Department of Fish and Game, Fish Bulletin 157, by Miller and Lea, or *Pacific Fishes of Canada,* Fisheries Research Board of Canada, Bulletin 180 by J. L. Hart. Much of the information here was found in these excellent sources. The drawings were taken from *Guide to the Coastal Marine Fishes of California.* For this source we are grateful to the California Department of Fish and Game and the authors.

Index

STARTER JIG KITS —
AVAILABLE BY MAIL ORDER

Handcrafted leadhead jigs in ½ to 8½ ounce sizes, epoxy painted heads, saltwater resistant hooks, with a selection of plastic worms and vinyl skirts are available by direct mail order from Sebastes Fisheries Company, P.O. Box 310, Kirkland, WA 98033.

For price list, mail a postcard with your address to:

Sebastes Fisheries Company
P.O. Box 310
Kirkland, WA. 98033